GENSHIKEN
OFFICIAL BOOK

EDITORIAL SUPERVISOR

KIO SHIMOKU

TRANSLATED BY

Satsuki Yamashita

ADAPTED BY

Ysabet Reinhart MacFarlane

LETTERING BY

Michaelis/Carpelis Design

BALLANTINE BOOKS NEW YORK

A Del Rey Trade Paperback Original

Genshiken Official Book copyright © 2004 by Kio Shimoku
English translation copyright © 2008 by Kio Shimoku

Published in the United States by Del Rey Books, an imprint of The Random House Publishing Group, a division of Random House, Inc., New York.

DEL REY is a registered trademark and the Del Rey colophon is a trademark of Random House, Inc.

Publication rights arranged through Kodansha Ltd.

First published in Japan in 2004 by Kodansha Ltd., Tokyo

ISBN 978-0-345-50402-9

Printed in the United States of America

WWW.DELREYMANGA.COM

9 8 7 6 5 4 3 2 1

Translator—Satsuki Yamashita
Adapter—Ysabet Reinhart MacFarlane
Lettering—Michaelis/Carpelis Design Assoc. Inc.

げんしけん OFFICIAL BOOK

THE SOCIETY FOR THE STUDY OF MODERN VISUAL CULTURE

監修 木尾士目

OFFICIAL BOOK

THE SOCIETY FOR THE STUDY OF MODERN VISUAL CULTURE

CONTENTS

1

Newbie Orientation

THE SOCIETY FOR THE STUDY OF MODERN VISUAL CULTURE

Shiiou University, just an hour's train ride from downtown, is the home of The Society for the Study of Modern Visual Culture, a club created by a group of lethargic otaku. What kind of club is it? you ask. And what do they do? Find out in this orientation!

A General-Purpose Otaku Club

HUMANS ARE CAPABLE OF FINDING A FAMILIAR IMAGE IN EVEN THE MOST ABSTRACT DRAWING.

THIS IS A BASIC FUNCTION OF THE HUMAN MIND.

"...DEFIES NATURAL ORDER."

"THE VERY EXISTENCE OF THE GENSHIKEN...

A General-Purpose Otaku Club

Appreciating all forms of visual culture as consumers, unrestricted by the limitations of genre

If you judge a club by its name, "The Society for the Study of Modern Visual Culture" sounds dry and academic. But in reality, this is a group of people who aim to appreciate manga, anime, and video games without being boxed in by preconceptions about each medium. Haraguchi, a sharp-tongued guy who belongs to the manga club as well as to the Genshiken, explains how the Genshiken was created—but at the same time, he criticizes its lack of focus.

Let's think about it. A similar thing has occurred as the martial arts have become more popular: Every college now has a club that studies the martial arts, even though there are also separate clubs devoted to karate, jujitsu, kickboxing, etc. The former type of club focuses on appreciating the martial arts as a whole, while the latter type practices specific styles. Why shouldn't otaku clubs follow similar patterns?

Members of manga or anime clubs tend to talk about manga and anime from the creator's perspective. But the Genshiken considers the consumer's point of view first. That's why they have such earnest debates about what they love about their favorite things.

Testing for Real Otaku

THERE'S GOTTA BE SOME PORN LYING AROUND HERE SOMEWHERE.

THAT'S RIGHT...

Club tradition: Spying on prospective members to see if they're true otaku

The Genshiken's members all share particular traits and feel that the club's reason for existence would be diluted if new members turned out to be "normal" people who lack the purity of the otaku mind, or fake otaku who want to join because it's the current fad.

It's also important to see if prospective members would be compatible with the club, since everyone's hobbies and obsessions will be under discussion. So each spring the newbies are tested: The club members leave them alone in the clubroom and then secretly watch to see what they do. If the new person does what Sasahara did and rummages around to find perverted fanzines to look through, he or she passes. (Ogiue fell for a similar trick when she reached for the yaoi fanzines that had been strategically placed on the table.)

The building layout makes this kind of surveillance possible. The Genshiken clubroom faces out onto a central garden, opposite the Children's Literature Club. Since the two clubs are on good terms, the Children's Literature Club lets the Genshiken borrow their window for spying.

Touring Akihabara

A wonderland that holds the three treasures of the Genshiken: Video Games, Manga, and Anime

For otaku who live near Tokyo, Akihabara (Akiba for short) is a paradise that never gets old. Shiiou University is only an hour west of the center of Tokyo, so the Genshiken members are able to visit Akiba from time to time.

Sometimes they go to look for rare fanzines in specialty stores; at other times they might visit cosplay cafés to admire the maids, or go in search of a place to buy an old computer at a dirt cheap price. If they were high-school students they would go home after shopping, but instead the Genshiken members end these excursions on a high note—karaoke, of course. The Genshiken rule is that only anime-related songs are allowed, out of respect for being in Akiba.

Shopping and karaoke are done for fun, but spending half the night lined up in a shopping arcade to wait for the midnight release of a new game is a *battle*!

They want to get the new game the minute it's available (more important, before anyone else!) and master it immediately. For a true gamer, that's real happiness. Take Madarame, for example, whose best jacket is his going-to-Akihabara outfit. It just demonstrates how strongly he thinks of Akiba as his sanctuary.

Comic-Fest

This otaku festival comes only twice a year. What draws them in? Is it just masochism?

Comic-Fest is held twice a year at the Tokyo Big Sight Convention Center in Ariake. It is the biggest fanzine exhibition and sale in Japan, and the Genshiken members spend hours in line for the chance to pick up the newest fanzines. Scorching heat and bitter cold aren't enough to keep them away.

As they wait, they resemble Indian mystics who willingly suffer to attain their goals. It's a test of mental discipline as well as physical endurance. Rumor has it that even triathlon athletes and veteran mountain climbers have proved unable to get through the long lines at Comic-Fest. But the new fanzines are so precious because of the hardships involved in getting them; it gives the perverted scenes within the fanzines' pages a special glow.

Sasahara's very first summer Comic-Fest started when he got off the first train at the International Exhibition Center station. It's against the rules for people to start lining up the night before the Fest, but the Tokyo Big Sight was already packed with people who came to buy fanzines and other otaku swag.

Madarame told Sasahara that the main hall was the battlefield. The members of the Genshiken consider themselves true otaku, and therefore the people who broke the rules and lined up overnight are amateurs. They inhabit completely different worlds.

Comic-Fest

KANJI STEPPED ABOARD WHAT WAS PERHAPS THE WORLD'S MOST OTAKU-FILLED TRAIN...

SHUT UP!

...
WHAT'RE YOU DOING HERE?

...AND HEADED FOR THE BIGGEST EVENT IN THE LIVES OF TOKYO OTAKU. DAY 3 OF THE HUGE SUMMER FAN-ZINE CONVENTION KNOWN AS "COMIC-FEST 2002."

I GUESS WE CAN F-FORGET ABOUT GETTING THE MOST POPULAR ZINES.

THIS COULD TAKE A WHILE.

THE LINE IS SO LONG. WE'RE GONNA HAVE TO COMPLETELY RE-THINK OUR BUYING STRATEGY.

PHEW

AUGUST 15TH (COMIC-FEST DAY 3)

THEY WERE EXTREMELY INEFFICIENT. AND AS EXPECTED, THEY HARDLY BOUGHT ANY OF THE BOOKS THAT THE GUYS HAD ASKED FOR.

SAKI TRICKED SASAHARA'S LITTLE SISTER INTO COMING ALONG. INSTEAD OF SPLITTING UP, SHE JUST FOLLOWED SAKI THE WHOLE TIME.

School Festival

PITARO THE MONSTER

ASTRO GIRL...

MAN OF STEEL...

GENSHIKEN EXHIBIT

FLASH

AS WE EXPECTED, OUR PUNISHMENT IS THAT WE WON'T BE ALLOWED TO PARTICIPATE IN THE SCHOOL FESTIVAL.

THEY'VE BEEN PASSED DOWN FROM GENERATION TO GENERATION.

FLASH FLASH

WE-WELL, THAT'S BECAUSE WE USE THEM EVERY YEAR.

IT KIND OF BUGS ME THAT THE POSTERS ARE BRITTLE AND YELLOW.

Their school festival exhibit is the exact same one that's been used every year since the Genshiken was created

At Shiiou University, the Genshiken is well known for its members' lack of drive, but if they don't participate in the autumn school festival they automatically lose their status as a recognized club, along with their club funding. To meet this requirement, they reuse the same overview of modern visual culture exhibit every year. This exhibit mainly consists of posters detailing some of the history of manga, anime, and games.

The exhibit has been handed down from generation to generation, so it's yellowed with age. It's reached the point where their habit of using these things created by their predecessors is now expected of them. The Genshiken is different from the anime and manga clubs, who invite guests and use the festival to announce their new projects.

Things changed a little when Ohno joined, giving them the chance to showcase her cosplay outfits and Tanaka's photographs. The basics of the exhibit are the same, but this addition gives the impression that they're an active club.

After the fire incident they were banned from participating in the festival, so they entered Kasukabe in the anime club's cosplay contest; they had to do *something*, or else their already tenuous club presence would disappear entirely.

The Daily "＿＿＿＿＿＿" Meeting

Every day the Genshiken has a meeting about whatever topic Madarame announces

One of the Genshiken's regular activities is the daily "(insert topic here)" meeting to discuss whatever Madarame comes up with. These meetings can cover anything and everything: "The 256th 'this week's Kujibiki Unbalance was awesome' meeting," "the 4th 'Kousaka isn't really an otaku, is he?' meeting," "the first 'let's summarize the Kuji-Un anime series' meeting," "the first-ever 'we've hardly got any pages done yet Comic-Fest strategy' meeting."...Once Madarame takes over, everything turns into a meeting.

They're called meetings, anyway, but there isn't much in the way of discussion or heated debate, and no one feels any need to come to a conclusion. Everyone sits at the table in the middle of the room and says whatever they want to; they don't do it to reach a conclusion, but to vent stress by expressing their feelings.

However, when Sasahara—the new president—and Kugayama—the artist— started arguing during the fanzine creation meeting, Madarame didn't know what to do. It was Kasukabe, the shadow power behind the presidential throne, who took care of the problem by taking stock of the situation and assigning tasks to each club member.

Creating a Fanzine

Creating a Fanzine

Overcoming obstacles to reach a goal brings its own kind of happiness

Let's use the experiences of a certain club we all know and love to outline the steps of creating a fanzine.

1) The group leader announces that a fanzine is in the works. 2) An application is filled out and submitted. 3) The Comic-Fest organization committee sends notification that the club can participate. 4) A sempai barges in and suggests trying to make money on the fanzine. This is the first obstacle to overcome. If you follow the moronic sempai's advice, everyone will be unhappy and the club will disintegrate. Don't forget that creating the fanzine is a club activity, not a scheme to turn a profit! 5) Establish a goal for when the work should be completed. 6) Even if you miss a deadline, it'll be all right if you pay the rush fee. 7) The club members start to argue over how slowly the fanzine is coming together. This is the second major obstacle. Conflict is inevitable if the group is divided between the people drawing the fanzine and the people making decisions. Getting through this stage requires a neutral voice to calmly guide things along. 8) Stay up late every night to make up for lost time. 9) Digitize the materials so they can be printed. 10) The completed fanzine is delivered to the exhibit hall. 11) Start selling. 12) Blow all of the proceeds on a party, since a celebration is obviously in order.

And that's how you create a fanzine!

Other Activities

Holidays and volunteer work are fun for a group!

The Genshiken members aren't in the club to educate others about their interests, but to enjoy everyday life to the fullest. That enjoyment is ultimately the Genshiken's main activity. Unlike sports clubs, arts and sciences clubs don't structure themselves around seniority, so their members don't have to be formal in the clubroom or when visiting one another's homes. Everyone in the Genshiken knows that the others are all otaku, too, so instead of hiding their hobbies they can talk openly about things like, say, their favorite porno games.

Once the entire club went to Kousaka's place to play games. The person with the most games is usually the one who winds up hosting. But in the summer they've been known to branch out by hitting the beach—Kugayama drove them down, and they sat under an umbrella and played "Gundam Shiritori". But the Genshiken members don't play only when they get together; for example, when they had to appeal to the school after the fire incident, they picked up trash and volunteered at several events. These also count as club activities.

Normal People

This generally refers to ordinary people, but there's a slightly different nuance being used here. Otaku use this term specifically when talking about non-otaku, and use "extraordinary people" to refer to themselves collectively.

Midnight Sale

Video games and other software sometimes go on sale right at midnight, just as the calendar rolls over to their release date. Putting them on sale in the middle of the night makes it possible for people to buy them immediately. This is especially common with popular porno games.

Garage Kit

Garage kits are a type of model kit designed so the final product can be displayed. They're more expensive than plastic models, and if they're designed by popular molders the price rises accordingly. A recent development is that some models are sold half-finished and prepainted.

"Girl Next Door" Character

The "girl next door" character is a recurring type of character in manga, anime, and video games. It simply means that the girl who lives next to you grows up to be really cute, and then falls in love with you. (Unfortunately, this isn't common in real life.)

Yurikamome

The Yurikamome line is public transit that runs from Shinbashi to Ariake, and is operated by computers. To otaku, it's a lifeline to their sanctuary: the Tokyo Big Sight.

Cosplay

"Cosplay," short for "costume play," refers to the hobby of dressing up as anime and manga characters. People who do this are called "cosplayers." They wear costumes at all kinds of events, not just at cosplay parties.

THE SOCIETY FOR THE STUDY OF MODERN VISUAL CULTURE

Genshiken Members Unite

During Sasahara's tenure as the Genshiken's third president, the club has nine regular members, plus the first president (who acts as an advisor) and two people who are connected to the club members. What happened after Sasahara joined the Genshiken? Let's look at the characters' profiles and relive some fond memories.

The Newbie Who Embraced His Inner Otaku at College

Kanji Sasahara

Born January 13   Capricorn   Blood type B

When Sasahara arrived at Shiiou University, he took the plunge and stopped hiding his otaku nature. This choice led him to The Society for the Study of Modern Visual Culture. Eventually, he becomes the third president.

★**Courage:** When Sasahara first stepped into Kousaka's room, he saw that Kousaka wasn't afraid of showing the world that he was an otaku. Sasahara realized he wanted to be equally brave about who he really was.

"WHAT I LACK IS THE COURAGE TO ACCEPT MYSELF FOR WHO I AM."

THE COF SERIES...YEAH, THESE CHARACTERS WERE PRETTY MUCH MADE FOR WHACKING OFF TO....

WOW, IT'S CHUN LIN! SHE'S STILL POPULAR, HA HA.

★**His first visit to a fanzine store:** Sasahara had been aware that such stores existed, but his very first visit to one was a profound experience for him.

Kanji Sasahara

I COULD BUY ONE OR TWO OF THE 2000 YEN BOOKS, OR FOUR OR FIVE OF THE ONES THAT ONLY COST A FEW HUNDRED YEN.

SHOULD I CHOOSE BASED ON THE ART, OR THE SERIES THE ZINE IS BASED ON...

I'VE GOTTA WEIGH MY OPTIONS...

I'VE REALLY STARTED TO BLEND IN.

I GUESS I'M JUST LIKE ALL THESE OTHER GUYS.

★**Weighing your options:** Fanzines are thin, but that doesn't mean they're cheap. You need to take several things into account when deciding, like your budget, the artwork, and the content.

★**Blending in:** This was only Sasahara's first Comic-Fest, but as soon as he relaxed he realized he fit in perfectly with the huge crowd of otaku.

INSTEAD OF PAYING MY RESPECTS AT THEIR GRAVES THIS YEAR, I CAME HERE.

UHH.... I SHOULD APOLOGIZE TO ALL MY ANCESTORS.

HERE'S 500-YEN BACK.

SOME... SOMETHING INSIDE ME IS OPENING UP...

I FEEL LIKE THE TOP OF MY HEAD IS GONNA BLOW.

SASAHARA-KUN!

I'M BUYING IT!

★**Apologizing to your ancestors:** Comic-Fest is held during the three days of Obon, so people attending the festival can't go back home to visit or pay their respects to their ancestors.

★**Opening up:** After Sasahara got comfortable with the other otaku, he went on a bit of a fanzine bender and bought a bunch of zines about the "Kuji-Un" president. Something inside him had started to open up.

★**A self-aware guy:** Sasahara's gone a bit out of control and started buying more otaku things, but since he's basically a humble guy he still has trouble openly calling himself an otaku.

★**"Monkey boy"?** Sasahara's little sister, Keiko, is what you might call a girly girl. She makes fun of her brother by calling him "monkey boy." High-school girls have always been the otaku's nemesis.

★**An otaku's girlfriend:** A girl dating an otaku is almost painful to watch. Sasahara's explanation painted a grim picture of Kasukabe's life.

★**Clearing your mind:** The key to surviving long lines is freeing yourself of distracting thoughts.

Kanji Sasahara

★**He's come a long way:** Sasahara used to be hesitant about doing things when he first joined the Genshiken. But now he's able to tell his friends to go home because he wants to play porno games. He's well on his way to being a fine otaku!

★**The new president:** When Sasahara succeeded Madarame and became the third president of the Genshiken, it was the first time he'd ever taken on that kind of responsibility.

I WANNA TASTE THE "TRUE PLEASURE OF PORN" RIGHT NOW!

HUH?

...SASAHARA.

YOU'RE TOO AFRAID...

THAT'S JUST A STUPID EXCUSE! YOU'VE NEVER EVEN TRIED TO MAKE IT AS A PRO!

I WOULD LIKE TO SEE US HAVE OUR OWN BOOTH AT THE NEXT COMIC-FEST.

★**Participating in Comic-Fest:** Caught up in his new role, Sasahara decided that they should participate in the next Comic-Fest. Little did he know that it would come back to haunt him...

★**Losing it:** Sasahara and Kugayama faced off over the fanzine's lack of progress. Sasahara's serious personality was a liability this time.

Harunobu Madarame

Born October 25   Scorpio   Blood type O

Madarame's behavior and attitude may not be the greatest, but his lifestyle as an otaku is unique. On the other hand, he tends to put too much energy into creating a persona for himself, while hiding his true self.

★**A snake in his past life:** Madarame is a guy who holds grudges, and he blames this on having been a snake in a past life.

BECAUSE I WAS A SNAKE IN MY PAST LIFE.

FLIP FLIP FLIP

NOT THAT AGAIN. ALWAYS WITH THE SNAKE...

JUST LOOK AT THE SPEED WITH WHICH HE SCANS THE LATEST ISSUE OF E.E. SAKURA.

UH...

★**Checking out new fanzines:** When they visit Akihabara, Madarame flips through the new fanzines so quickly that his hands are a blur. It's a highly developed skill.

YOU DON'T JUST TAKE OFF HER CLOTHES...

YOU SCREW HER TOO.

★**Freak:** Madarame made a disturbing comment about screwing Lolitas in porno games. He exaggerates his perversity when he's around Kasukabe. Is he trying to keep her from seeing who he really is?

Harunobu Madarame

★**Military otaku:** Haraguchi blithely says that the Genshiken has no reason for existing, and dismisses Madarame as a military otaku wannabe who only knows about Zeon army.

COMRADES! STAND UP AND FIGHT...

HUMANS ARE CAPABLE OF FINDING A FAMILIAR IMAGE IN EVEN THE MOST ABSTRACT DRAWING.

EXACTLY!

...BUT ALL HE DOES IS REPEAT WHAT HE'S HEARD ON GUNDAM. HE DOESN'T REALLY KNOW ANYTHING.

AND MADARAME TALKS LIKE HE'S A REAL MILITARY OTAKU...

★**Theorizing:** Madarame described how the brain works in an effort to explain why otaku can be turned on by 2-D characters.

WIGGLE WIGGLE

SPLASH SPLASH

I'VE GOT ALL THIS ADRENALIN, I'M STARTING TO GET A RUNNER'S HIGH. I'M ON MY WAY TO ENLIGHTEN-MENT.

Runner's high: At Comic-Fest, the long wait in the rain eventually gave Madarame a runner's high that turned his suffering into an adrenaline rush.

BUY TWO COPIES OF THE GOOD ONES.

DON'T COME. STAY HERE, AND BUY FAN-ZINES.

★**Carried out on a stretcher:** When he injured his arm, Madarame told the other Genshiken members to go buy fanzines instead of accompanying him. A legend was born.

★Madarame, the second president: The Genshiken's first president held that post for many years, but finally had Madarame take his place.

SO, I'D LIKE TO RECOMMEND THAT MADARAME-KUN BECOME THE NEXT COMMANDER IN CHIEF.

WHOA, THAT'S A PRETTY HARD-CORE STATEMENT.

THERE'S NO WAY THAT YOU COULD REALLY HAVE A LITTLE SISTER.

★No way you could have a little sister: When Madarame learned that Sasahara had a younger sister, he insisted that it was impossible.

★Favorite game: Madarame's new favorite form of sexual harassment is leaving porn game magazines lying on the table in the Genshiken room. Is this some subtle form of revenge against women's failure to understand him?

RIGHT NOW, HE'S SHOPPING FOR "A BUNCH OF PORN GAME MAGAZINES TO PUT ON THE GENSHIKEN TABLE."

...AT LEAST THAT'S HIS EXCUSE FOR BUYING ALL THESE MAGAZINES.

LATELY MADARAME HAS BEEN ENJOYING A NEW FORM OF SEXUAL HARASSMENT.

THERE'S NO REASON I SHOULD BE SO NERVOUS AROUND KASUKABE-SAN. I MEAN, IT'S NOT LIKE SHE'S A "LOLITA" GIRL OR ANYTHING.

SHE SHOULD BE THE ONE WHO FEELS UNCOMFORTABLE, NOT ME. GOD, I'M SO WEAK.

★Pedophile: Lolita girls are Madarame's "type," rather than normal girls, but he still can't help being nervous when he's alone with Kasukabe.

★Reality can never live up to a video game: Madarame came right out with the truth—"Even if he has a girlfriend, he's still gonna play porn games!"

WHY?

THEY'RE TWO TOTALLY SEPARATE THINGS!

NO WAY! IMPOSSIBLE! EVEN IF HE HAS A GIRLFRIEND, HE'S STILL GONNA PLAY PORN GAMES!

ISN'T IT OBVIOUS? REALITY CAN NEVER LIVE UP TO A VIDEO GAME!

UH-OH.

Harunobu Madarame

★**Madarame's room:** After the fire incident, the Genshiken didn't have anywhere to meet. When it was Madarame's turn to have the club hang out in his room, he didn't bother cleaning up first.

WHY IS IT THIS PLACE LOOKS SO MUCH DIFFERENT FROM KOUSAKA'S ROOM?

HA, HA, HA! THIS IS MY ROOM IN ITS NATURAL STATE!

YOU COULD AT LEAST PICK UP THE GARBAGE AND DIRTY LAUNDRY.

HOW RUDE.

AT LEAST PUT AWAY THAT STUFF...

THE PORN...

HE BOUGHT THESE PHOTOS FROM A BUDDING PAPARAZZI.

★**His hobby?:** When Kasukabe snooped through Madarame's drawer, she found some S&M porn DVDs— of real people, not anime.

★**Secret:** The DVDs Kasukabe found were a decoy to keep her from learning Madarame's real secret: that he had pictures of her cosplaying.

DO YOU HAVE TO LAUGH LIKE THAT?

OH, COME ON...WHAT'S WITH THOSE SQUARE GLASSES?

HA, HA, HA.

Time for a change: When Madarame went job hunting, he bought more fashionable square-framed glasses. Kasukabe cracked up when she saw him.

Makoto Kousaka

Born February 2   Aquarius   Blood type B

Kousaka has the face of a teen idol, but inside,
he's otaku to the bone.
No one else even comes close to beating him at fight games.

HAVE A SEAT.

★His room: Kousaka's room shows off just how serious an otaku he is. He brought everything with him from home, and a close look shows that he has porn game and Lolita characters on his walls.

★Blunt: Kousaka went shopping with Kasukabe, but then headed off to Akihabara to meet up with the Genshiken members. He doesn't really understand what girls want, does he?

I SURE DO.

YEP.

★When Kousaka was younger: Kousaka had his head shaved when he was younger. When he and Kasukabe met up again in college, she was surprised at how different he looked—and she fell in love with him.

Makoto Kousaka

★**Oblivious:** Kousaka is always cheerful, and arrives at the Genshiken singing anime songs loudly. Someone who lives completely in his own world is very strong, somehow.

"MY FIRST KISS" ♡ ♪

WHAT'S UP WITH HIM?

BUT HE DOESN'T LOOK, TALK OR ACT LIKE ANY OTAKU I'VE EVER SEEN. WHAT A WEIRDO.

I MEAN, IF YOU GO BY WHAT HE'S INTO, HE'S A TOTAL OTAKU.

★**Haraguchi's opinion:** Even the sharp-tongued Haraguchi couldn't find much to say about the apparent gap between Kousaka's appearance and his hobbies.

★**Undefeated:** Kousaka participated in the fight game tournament the anime club hosted at the school festival, and he effortlessly blew the competition away. The prize was a 25-year supply of lame video games.

I KNOW, RIGHT?

HE'S CONSTANTLY REDEFINING EXPECTATIONS. HE'S LIKE MICHAEL SCHUMACHER.

I'D HEARD THE RUMORS, BUT KOUSAKA-KUN REALLY IS AMAZING.

NO ONE CAN EVEN TOUCH HIM.

YOU LOOK SO CUTE, SAKI-CHAN.

★**Soothing:** Kasukabe can easily tear strips off the guys, but even she has her teary moments. At times like that, Kousaka is able to comfort her.

★**Unmoving:** The more action there is on the screen, the less master gamer Kousaka's eyes move. Maybe it's one of his secrets to winning.

WHEN KOUSAKA GETS REALLY INTO A GAME, HIS EYES STOP MOVING.

CLICK CLICK CLICK

CLACK CLACK CLICK

CLACK CLACK CLACK

CLICK CLICK CLICK

I'VE BEEN LOOKING FORWARD TO IT ALL DAY.

★**Interruption:** Kousaka realized that Kasukabe needed some affection, so he gave her a hug. But he stopped when the anime he wanted to see came on. Kousaka would take anime over sex any day.

WHOA! THAT COMBO ATTACK WAS COOL.

HUH? HOW CAN HE BLOCK ALL THREE OF MY ATTACK'S?

NOW HE'S GONNA THROW ME DOWN.

CLICK CLICK CLICK

★**A world apart:** Newbies who want to join the Genshiken have to play fight games against Kousaka. These guys came in feeling confident about their skill, but Kousaka completely obliterated them.

YOU MIGHT WANNA KEEP IT DOWN A LITTLE. YOU DON'T WANT TO CAUSE A SCENE.

★**Reliable:** Kousaka's grip on reality seems a little flimsy, but he can still tell when to step in. He's completely different from Madarame, who talks big but runs away the moment he senses danger.

Makoto Kousaka

YOU REALLY GET TO SEE THE PROCESS OF HOW THE MAIN CHARACTER FALLS IN LOVE WITH THE FEMALE CHARACTERS.

I LIKE THAT GAME BECAUSE...

★Tough: Information is a key part of the otaku arsenal. Kousaka can talk all night if porno games are the subject at hand. He's truly a paragon among otaku.

THERE'S NO WAY I COULD EVER QUIT PLAYING PORN GAMES.

★No way: Kasukabe would like to be in denial about how much of an otaku Kousaka is, but it's impossible when he cheerfully says things like, "There's no way I could ever quit playing porn games."

DON'T DO ANYTHING YOU MIGHT REGRET.

★The last frontier: Kousaka told Kasukabe that she probably didn't want to know about Madarame's real hobby.

IT TOOK ME A LITTLE LONGER THAN I THOUGHT IT WOULD TO DO MY MAKEUP.

I LEARNED BY WATCHING SAKI-CHAN.

★Enthusiastic: Kousaka volunteered to cosplay as a female character from "Kuji-Un" to boost sales of their fanzine.

Saki Kasukabe

Born July 19   Cancer   Blood type AB

Kasukabe usually has no time for otaku, but she joined the Genshiken because of her boyfriend. She's the only person in the club with a normal person's sensibilities.

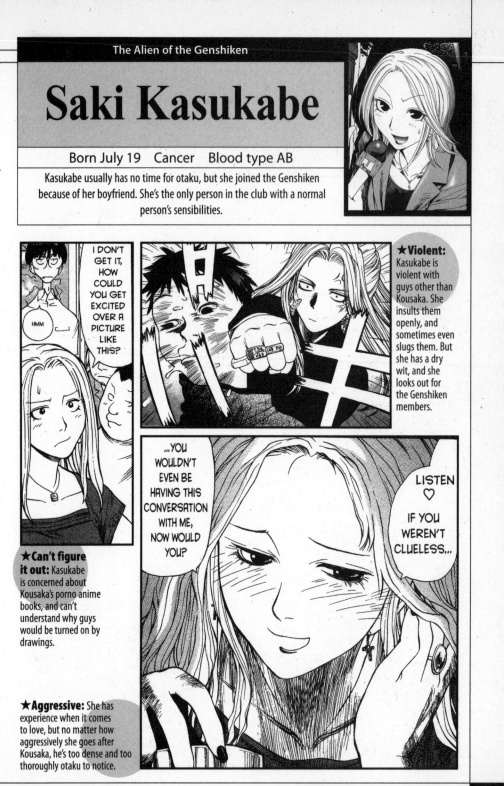

I DON'T GET IT, HOW COULD YOU GET EXCITED OVER A PICTURE LIKE THIS?

HMM

★**Violent:** Kasukabe is violent with guys other than Kousaka. She insults them openly, and sometimes even slugs them. But she has a dry wit, and she looks out for the Genshiken members.

...YOU WOULDN'T EVEN BE HAVING THIS CONVERSATION WITH ME, NOW WOULD YOU?

LISTEN ♡ IF YOU WEREN'T CLUELESS...

★**Can't figure it out:** Kasukabe is concerned about Kousaka's porno anime books, and can't understand why guys would be turned on by drawings.

★**Aggressive:** She has experience when it comes to love, but no matter how aggressively she goes after Kousaka, he's too dense and too thoroughly otaku to notice.

Saki Kasukabe

★**Can't believe it:** Kasukabe was shocked to discover that some otaku are girls. She's interested in figuring Ohno out.

★**Ex-boyfriend:** The guy Kasukabe dated before Kousaka looks hip and shallow—nothing at all like the Genshiken members.

★**Out of place:** Kasukabe's fashion sense may not stand out in Shibuya or Roppongi, but it catches the eye at Comic-Fest, home to the highest density of otaku in Japan.

★**Explosion:** Madarame put cat ears on Kasukabe's head, just in time for her ex to see her. Kousaka calmed her down a little, but she still wound up blowing up over it.

IT'S "PUYOPUYO" COSPLAY.

I'M JOINING!

★**Joining Genshiken:** The first president saw Kasukabe being a little naughty in the clubroom, and subtly blackmailed her into joining the Genshiken.

★**"Puyopuyo":** Kasukabe realized that video games were the way to Kousaka's heart. After they played "Puyopuyo," she tried to cosplay as a puyopuyo for him.

★**Modesty? What modesty?:** Madarame claimed that being turned on by porn games requires advanced intellectual capacity. Kasukabe countered by saying that players are still just jerking off.

ADVANCED INTELLECTUAL CAPACITY? YOU'RE SO FULL OF SHIT! ALL YOU'RE DOING IS GRABBING YOUR WANG AND JERKING OFF!

★**Nose hair:** One afternoon Kasukabe was reading in the Genshiken room when Madarame thought he saw a hair in her nose. Whether it was really a nose hair or not is still a mystery.

Saki Kasukabe

★**Fire!:** Kasukabe was daydreaming about burning the Genshiken's trash when she dropped her cigarette and really set it on fire.

★**Crying her way out:** To make up for the fire, Kasukabe was told she had to cosplay in the contest in Ohno's place. But her usual tough attitude kept her attempt at tears from working.

DRIP

DO I REALLY HAVE TO DO IT?

DID YOU MAKE YOUR COSTUME YOURSELF?

OH, NO...

NO, A FRIEND MADE IT FOR ME.

THEY'RE TAKING PICTURES OF ME.

★**President:** Kasukabe's first cosplay was of the "Kuji-Un" president, the helmeted Kettenkrad. It turned out to be an ideal choice for her, and she was a big hit.

★**Cleansing:** Before Kasukabe went to see the Genshiken's fanzine, she took a shower to purify herself. She truly is the president behind the scenes!

Souichiro Tanaka

Born December 22 Capricorn Blood type AB

Tanaka is the most skilled Genshiken member.
He can sew cosplay outfits as well as make plastic models
and garage kits.

★The odd man out: Tanaka used to be a member of the anime club, but he left to join the Genshiken because the anime club didn't put any money into cosplay.

HEY TANAKA, DIDN'T YOU LEAVE THE ANIME CLUB TO COME HERE?

HER FACE, HER BODY, EVEN HER NAME, "AOI," SEEM COMMONPLACE, AND YET THE FAMILIARITY IS ALLURING.

SHE'S GOT THAT "GIRL NEXT DOOR" KIND OF PERSONALITY TOO AND YET SHE'S A STRONG WOMAN...

THIS CHARACTER WAS DEFINITELY DESIGNED TO HAVE MASS APPEAL.

YEAH, CAUSE THEY WEREN'T WILLING TO BUDGET ANY OF THEIR MONEY FOR COSPLAY.

THIS FIGURE WAS MADE WITH THE IDEA OF SHOWING HER IN AN "OLD-FASHIONED, TIGHT FITTING SCHOOL UNIFORM," AND THAT DRAMATICALLY CHANGES OUR PRECONCEIVED NOTIONS OF HER AS A "GIRL NEXT DOOR" TYPE.

★In-depth knowledge: Tanaka explained the appeal of garage kits to Sasahara. He began by explaining the character's name, and worked up to her role in the show and her attributes.

Souichiro Tanaka

★**Photographer:** At Comic-Fest, Tanaka doubles as a photographer and takes pictures of cosplayers. His cyber alias is FUKUROU.

HERE'S A PICTURE OF YOU FROM LAST TIME.

WOW, CAN I REALLY HAVE IT? THANKS SO MUCH, FUKUROU-SAN.*

★**Principle:** Tanaka believes it's wrong for people to comment on how cute a cosplayer is if they don't even know the original character. That's the key distinction between a cosplay outfit and regular clothes.

THAT'S PART OF COS-PLAY.

YOU WON'T GET IT UNLESS YOU KNOW THE CHARACTER SHE'S PLAYING.

AND I'D SWEAR TO NEVER EVER TELL ANYONE ELSE WHAT HER MEASURE-MENTS ARE.

ACTUALLY, I FIGURED I'D HAVE YOU TAKE CARE OF THAT, KASUKABE-SAN.

WHAT DO YOU THINK? WILL WE GET IN TROUBLE IF WE START WALKING AROUND?

HMM, THAT MIGHT BE A MORAL VIOLATION OF THE COSPLAY CODE.

★**The rule:** People who make cosplay outfits never betray the cosplayers' measurements. If a cosplayer accuses you of breaking their confidence, your career is over.

★**Orthodox:** Cosplay has its own code of conduct. It's not about wearing whatever you want and walking around casually.

★**The way of plastic models:** Girls may see plastic models as simple toys, but the effort involved in making them gives models a soul that toys lack, and makes them more appealing.

★**A terrible fiend?:** Kasukabe broke one of Tanaka's plastic models by being too rough with it. This was one of those rare times when Tanaka got upset.

★**Just like King Arthur:** Tanaka knows about props as well as cosplay outfits. He took the sword that's been passed down in the Genshiken and...

★**Behold the power!:** Tanaka was able to figure out Kasukabe's measurements just from seeing her in a bathing suit. He was only off by a few inches, which reinforced his pride and confidence as an artisan.

Souichiro Tanaka

YOU'VE EVEN GOT A HIGH-TECH SEWING MACHINE.

★**A career plan:** Kasukabe plans to open a boutique after graduation. She sees Tanaka as a valuable potential partner because he can design and sew.

NOPE. I DON'T HAVE ONE OF THOSE.

A LIFE-SIZE ACTION FIGURE?

YOU KNOW, ONE OF THOSE LIFE-SIZE FIGURES.

KOUSAKA SHOWED ME ONE IN A MAGAZINE.

★**Well-loved machine:** Tanaka keeps a sewing machine in his room to make cosplay outfits. The machine is his partner, allowing him to create a stream of masterpieces.

★**Accusation:** Kasukabe accused Tanaka of having a life-size figure to use for cosplay.

★**"Jackpot!"** There are completed plastic models as well as rare porno game garage kits in Tanaka's closet.

★**Chance meeting:** While Sasahara was walking around Akihabara, he bumped into Tanaka and Ohno. The cosplaying couple fit right in in the otaku capital.

THAT'S ALL RIGHT. I HAD A LATE BREAK-FAST.

WE WERE GONNA GO GRAB SOME LUNCH. WANNA COME?

HA, HA. OH, WALKING AROUND, EH?

JUST WALKING AROUND.

Kanako Ohno

Born July 14   Cancer   Blood type O

Ohno's cosplay hobby single-handedly broadened the Genshiken's horizons. She brightens up every event they participate in. Kasukabe picks on her even more than the others, because the two of them have completely opposite interests and personalities.

★ Back from abroad: Starting in third grade, Ohno lived in Boston for about 10 years. Her English is excellent.

I'M KANAKO OHNO.

NICE TO MEET YOU GUYS.

BALDING, MIDDLE-AGED GUYS WITH SUNGLASSES...

HA HA!

IT IS TOTALLY WEIRD THOUGH.

★ Bald guys in sunglasses: Ohno decorates her room with anime posters of balding older men. Being able to assert your tastes is fundamental to being an otaku.

I GUESS IT IS PRETTY WEIRD.

BUT THEY'RE SO COOL.

★**Strength:** When Kasukabe found out that Ohno liked bald men, Ohno choked her. Even Kasukabe couldn't break her hold.

★**Alien:** Ohno cosplayed as part of the Genshiken exhibit at the school festival. She played her part perfectly, but Kasukabe said she looked like an alien.

★**Pleasure:** Ohno tries to explain the pleasure of cosplay to Kasukabe, but the cultural divide is too wide.

★**People take pictures:** She's usually shy and reserved, but when Ohno gets on-stage she changes dramatically. It's one of cosplay's great mysteries.

★**A dream come true:** Ohno spent most of her childhood in the U.S., but she knew about Comic-Fest from her friends in Japan. This was the moment her dream came true.

SAKI-SAN.

OH MY GOD... I GUESS YOU WOULD NEED A BRA THAT BIG FOR THOSE SUPERHERO-SIZED BOOBS.

SHIVER

D?

DOUBLE D?

★**Soccer balls:** According to a study, girls who wish their boobs were bigger don't get them; instead, impressive figures go to girls who don't care.

★**Embarrassment:** When she heard about Kasukabe's "friend" whose boyfriend had doggie-style sex with her while watching anime, Ohno commented about it lasting for 30 minutes and embarrassed herself.

YOU'RE TRYING TO HIDE YOUR EMBARRASS-MENT, BUT IT AIN'T WORKING.

THAT'S PRETTY AMAZING THAT HE LASTED THIRTY MINUTES.

★**Keeps on trying:** Ohno never stops trying to get Kasukabe to cosplay with her. She thinks being in a cosplay duo would be fun.

OH YEAH.

YEAH, BUT... I WANT TO TAKE ADVANTAGE OF EVERY OPPORTUNITY I GET.

WILL YOUR PERSONALITY TOTALLY CHANGE WHEN I ASK IF WE START TALKING ABOUT COSPLAY.

WHEN HELL FREEZES OVER!

★**The bait:** Ohno cosplayed as a maid to draw in prospective members. Maid outfits are nothing new, but they're popular on her because they show off her huge boobs.

NO PHOTOS PLEASE GENSHIKEN

AH...

I CAN'T STOP..

★**The tears keep coming:** Ohno said it was okay when Kasukabe accidentally broke the plastic model she'd worked on for a week, but she couldn't keep from crying.

Kanako Ohno

★"I want you to do cosplay": When Kasukabe asked Ohno how she could make up for breaking the plastic model, there was only one thing Ohno wanted.

I WANT YOU TO DO COSPLAY.

UH...

WELL... AT LEAST LET GO OF MY HAND.

★No sense of coordination: Ohno wore a polka-dotted Lolita kind of swimsuit to the beach. She fell down as soon as a wave hit her.

MY BUTT GOT ALL WET.

★Cosplay shows more skin: Ohno is okay with showing her skin when she's cosplaying, but she's embarrassed by wearing a swimsuit.

★The fabled yaoi fanzines: When Sasahara's sister was curious about porn fanzines, Ohno tried to show her some yaoi ones for women.

I HAVE SOME REALLY GOOD ONES THAT ARE MEANT FOR GIRLS.

YEAH, A LOT OF PEOPLE FROM THE MANGA CLUB ARE GONNA BE IN THE CONTEST TOO.

OF COURSE, THE REAL CENTER OF ATTENTION WILL BE *YOKO-SAN.

ISN'T THAT WHAT THEY'RE SAYING?

BUT THEY WANT TO GET AS MANY STUDENTS AS THEY CAN TO JOIN THE CONTEST.

★Using a different name: Much like Tanaka uses the name FUKUROU, Ohno uses "Yoko-san" as her cosplay name.

WE WOULD NEVER DO ANYTHING THAT WOULD SOIL THE INTEGRITY OF THE CHARACTER.

★Preserving the character's integrity: When Kasukabe asked if Ohno had sex in costume, Ohno gave the above reply.

★Wrong: There's more to cosplay than wearing outfits. Part of the process is understanding and becoming one with the character.

BUT WAIT...IF SHE DOES JOIN THE CONTEST WITHOUT FULLY UNDERSTANDING HER CHARACTER, SHE'D BE BREAKING ONE OF THE PRIMARY LAWS OF COSPLAY...MAYBE SHE'D BE BETTER OFF NOT DOING IT AT ALL...

THEN AGAIN...

OF COURSE, I MIGHT NEVER GET THE CHANCE TO SEE SAKI DO COSPLAY AGAIN.

YOU'LL BARELY HAVE TIME TO READ ALL MY RESEARCH AND I'M TOO SICK TO REALLY...

MUMBLE MUMBLE

MUMBLE MUMBLE MUMBLE

I WAS HOPING TO REALLY COACH YOU ABOUT HOW TO PORTRAY THE TRUE ESSENCE OF YOUR COSPLAY CHARACTER.

TO REALLY GET YOU INTO CHARACTER, I'D NEED AT LEAST THREE WEEKS...ONE WEEK JUST ISN'T ENOUGH.

PROBABLY THE BEST STRATEGY FOR YOU WOULD BE TO GO OUT THERE WITH THE ATTITUDE "I DON'T KNOW MUCH ABOUT COSPLAY, BUT THIS COSTUME WAS SO CUTE I THOUGHT I'D GIVE IT A TRY."

★Beginner's charm: Veteran cosplayers have their charm, but there's a special something about novices.

THERE'S NO SUCH THING AS A GIRL WHO HATES QUEERS!

★Words of wisdom: Ohno got fed up with Ogiue's attitude and screamed that "there's no such thing as a girl who hates queers!" Otaku wisdom for the ages!

WOW!

THEY'RE REALLY DOING IT.

★Two birds with one stone: When the Genshiken participated in Comic-Fest as a circle for the first time, Ohno cosplayed as the vice president both to lure in customers and to scratch her own cosplay itch.

NOT THAT I COULD EVER REALLY BE A CRIMINAL.

NO, BUT FOR SOME REASON WHEN I PUT THIS ON, IT MAKES ME FEEL LIKE A CRIMINAL MASTERMIND. EVER SINCE LAST YEAR'S SCHOOL FESTIVAL.

★Criminal mastermind: For no real reason, Ohno wore a mask when she was spying on Ogiue. She wanted to feel like a criminal mastermind.

A Kind, Easygoing Guy

Mitsunori Kugayama

Born June 29　Cancer　Blood type A

Kugayama is chunky and reserved, and
doesn't like standing out in a crowd. He does tend to get irritated
when things don't go his way, though.

M-MADARAME IS JUST TRYING TO CREATE A CHARACTER, DON'T TAKE HIM TOO SERIOUSLY.

YOU'RE REALLY STUCK ON THAT PHRASE, AREN'T YOU?

★ **Soft voice:** Kugayama's voice is low and indistinct, so he tries to avoid talking outdoors. Cashiers usually have a hard time hearing him.

★ **Understanding:** Kugayama understands how Madarame thinks. When Madarame kept repeating the same line, Kugayama told Sasahara that it was just how Madarame creates a "character" for himself.

HE BUYS EVERY "SISTER ANGEL" ZINE THAT HE CAN GET HIS HANDS ON.

HE CHOOSES SOLELY BASED ON THE ORIGINAL SERIES.

HE LIKES "SISTER ANGEL."

I'VE DECIDED NEVER TO TALK IN SITUATIONS LIKE THIS.

★ **Individual strategies:** When buying fanzines, Tanaka bases his decisions on the artists, while Kugayama goes by their content. The former method gives you a better chance of getting high-quality fanzines.

★Surprise: Kugayama has such unexpectedly high-quality furniture that Kasukabe couldn't help wondering if he came from a rich family.

★A nice guy: When the group decided to go to the beach, Kugayama offered to drive. Once they got there, he opted to watch everyone's stuff while he rested up for the drive home.

★Secret art collection: There's a secret collection of porn art in Kugayama's closet. He seems happy when it gets praised.

★Knowing yourself: Kugayama is the only Genshiken member who can draw, but he has enough self-awareness to realize he doesn't have what it takes to go pro.

★**Avoiding responsibility:** Kugayama always wanted to make a doujinshi, but he figured that the person who suggested it would have to be responsible for it, so he was waiting for someone else to bring it up.

I-I FIGURED IF I SUGGESTED IT, THEN I'D HAVE TO BE THE ONE WHO TOOK RESPONSIBILITY FOR EVERYTHING.

I'M OUT THERE TRYING TO GET A REAL JOB.

T-TANAKA IS JUST GOING TO A FASHION DESIGN SCHOOL, AND M-MADARAME ISN'T REALLY DOING ANYTHING AT ALL, BUT...

★**Looking for a job:** Kugayama wants to find a nice job, but that's no excuse for not working on the fanzine.

★**Trust:** When Tanaka and Ohno began a relationship, Kugayama was the only person they told. They must trust his ability to keep a secret.

TH-THEY'RE GOING OUT, RIGHT? I KNOW.

★**Not my fault:** Kugayama dislikes out-and-out arguing, so he tends to try pinning flimsy excuses on other people.

HMMPH! THERE'S NOTHING W-WORSE THAN AN EDITOR WHO KILLS HIS ARTIST'S PASSION.

A Girl Who Jumps Out of Buildings

Chika Ogiue

Born March 28　Aries　Blood type A

Ogiue is a feisty girl who used to be in the manga club.
She has a somewhat complicated mind-set, since she's an otaku
who claims to hate otaku.

AND NOW YOU WANT TO PAWN HER OFF ON US?

THE CLUB ITSELF WAS PROBABLY RESPONSIBLE FOR THE REMAINING 10%.

I'D SAY THE NEW GIRL WAS PROBABLY ABOUT 90% AT FAULT.

★**Transferring in:** Ogiue's...spirited... personality caused conflict when she was in the manga club. It's about 90 percent her fault.

I WANTED THEM TO FEEL GUILTY.

THAT'S SO TYPICAL.

OUCH...

★**Suicide attempt?:**
When Ogiue arrived at the Genshiken, her left arm was in a sling. She'd jumped out a window to spite the members of the manga club.

Chika Ogiue

★Battle of the girls: Ogiue looks like a total otaku, but she claims to hate otaku girls. Her attitude irritates Ohno a little.

★Trauma: Ogiue says that girls who like yaoi are sick, but she herself saw her first yaoi fanzine when she was in the fifth grade.

★Back against the wall: After Kuchiki spotted Ogiue at a yaoi event, she tried to convince the club that her brother had asked her to go, but...

★The second attempt: Ogiue tried to jump out of the building again when Ohno gave her a meaningful smile. It's an interesting way of escaping reality.

★Baggy clothes: Kasukabe immediately figured out that Ogiue was wearing men's clothes to hide her figure.

NOW LET'S TAKE A LOOK AT YOUR OUTFIT. STAND UP FOR A SECOND.

UH... I JUST LIKE WEARING BAGGY CLOTHES.

THIS IS WAY TOO BIG FOR YOU. IS THIS A MEN'S SIZE?

★Formerly in the manga club: When she heard that the Genshiken was making a fanzine, she began sketching. Simple illustrations are a piece of cake for an ex–manga club member.

HMM...

MY VISION IS ACTUALLY REALLY BAD.

YEAH, BUT I JUST STARTED THIS SPRING.

★Changing her looks: Ogiue has bad eyes, so she started wearing contacts when she came to college. That's also when she switched to her distinctive "paintbrush" hairstyle.

-DUM

★Oops: Even when she tries wearing fashionable clothes, she's still obviously an otaku. Kasukabe, who knows what Ogiue's really like, couldn't stand seeing her dressed like that.

Chika Ogiue

★**Dialect:** When Ogiue gets excited or moved, she switches back to her Tohoku dialect. It might be a turn-on for otaku who are into that kind of thing.

★**Wanting to help:** When she heard that the fanzine was behind schedule and offered to draw pages, could it be that she wanted to help Sasahara?

★**Sad:** Ogiue doesn't like seeing the Genshiken members fight, especially after they took her in.

Manabu Kuchiki

Born March 21 Aries Blood type B

Kuchiki is an insensitive guy who yells at girls, screams completely random nonsense, and has no sense of delicacy. It all adds up to Kasukabe punching him a lot.

★**A boomerang member:** Kuchiki had tried to join the Genshiken before, but Kousaka's game skills scared him off. He joined the anime club, but came back to the Genshiken a year later.

★**Intimidation:** Kuchiki gets upset at the littlest things, and sometimes pretends to attack Kasukabe or Ogiue.

Manabu Kuchiki

★Sneaking shots: Kuchiki took a picture of Ogiue at a yaoi event when she wasn't looking. Kasukabe called him on it (and punished him) in front of everyone.

★A crushing blow: Kuchiki tapped Ogiue on the head and was immediately beaten down by Kasukabe.

★The lowest of the low: Being around women doesn't keep Kuchiki from reading porn openly. He's definitely the worst kind of bastard.

★Perfect timing: When Kasukabe saw Kousaka cross-dressing, she was at a loss for words. Kuchiki broke the tension in the air.

★Tough: Kuchiki always gets back up no matter how hard he's shoved down, then acts like nothing happened. He's mentally and physically tough.

First President

Name, birth date, and personal info are unknown

The first president has been president since anyone can remember. He's been around the Genshiken since 1987. He doesn't exactly radiate a strong presence.

★Melancholy: When he says something as simple as, "It sure is windy out there," the words somehow reveal the weight of the years he's been supporting the Genshiken.

IT SURE IS WINDY OUT THERE.

AAHH!

WELL, I'VE GOT SOME- THING THAT MIGHT HELP.

★Stealth: The first president doesn't just lack a sense of presence—he also pops up out of nowhere. He can materialize right behind people with no warning. Could the Genshiken room have a secret passage?

First President

★ **How old is he?:** When the gang found a newsletter from 1987, they discovered that the president had been president even then. How old *is* he?

WAIT! HOW OLD IS THE ORIGINAL PREZ?

OKAY, LET'S SAY I WAS "DOING THAT"...

...DON'T YOU THINK I'D HAVE PLENTY OF DIRT ON OTHER PEOPLE, MALE OR FEMALE, WHO HAVE DONE THINGS SO NASTY THAT IF WORD GOT OUT THEY WOULD'VE DROPPED OUT OF SCHOOL LONG AGO....?

BUT CAN YOU THINK OF ANYBODY WHO HAS ACTUALLY DROPPED OUT?

★ **Peeping:** The first president knows secrets about a lot of people. Kasukabe accused him of having hidden cameras around the campus, but he responded by bringing up what she and Kousaka were doing in the Genshiken clubroom.

★ **Informed:** After Kasukabe started the fire, she went to the former president to ask his advice. According to his information, the Genshiken wasn't in danger of being shut down.

BUT ACCORDING TO WHAT I'VE HEARD...

THEY'RE NOT GONNA COMPLETELY SHUT US DOWN.

I'M RIGHT OVER HERE.

★ **Succession of power:** The rumor about the first president never graduating was true. But this year he is writing his graduation thesis, and chose Madarame to take his place.

Haraguchi

あははははは

HA HA HA HA

SORRY, BUT MADARAME AND THE REST OF YOU GUYS AREN'T WELCOME.

IS THAT RIGHT?

★**Self-centered and selfish:** Haraguchi dropped by the Genshiken when they were having problems and tried to steal Kousaka and Ohno away.

★**Ear to the ground:** When the Genshiken decided to participate in Comic-Fest, Haraguchi barged in and started barking orders.

TCH, WELL, THAT'S NOTHING MORE THAN MASTURBATION.

YOU COULD GET THEM ALL TO COLLABORATE ON A KUJI-UN BOOK.

I WAS THINKING... HOW ABOUT IF I INTRODUCE YOU TO A BUNCH OF FAMOUS DOUJINSHI ARTISTS, AND...

★**Masturbation:** Sasahara wanted to create a fanzine as a Genshiken club activity, but Haraguchi's only thoughts were about profit.

B-B-B-BASTARD!!

YOU CAN KEEP IT.

¥500

★**Jinxed:** After Sasahara turned down Haraguchi's offer to hook them up with famous doujinshi artists, Haraguchi flipped through the Genshiken fanzine and dismissed it completely.

Keiko Sasahara

Born June 10   Gemini   Blood type A

Keiko is Sasahara's younger sister, who fell in love with Kousaka.
She's so different from Sasahara that you'd swear there was no way they
could have grown up together.

★**Heavy makeup:**
Keiko wears so much makeup that you can't tell what she really looks like. She's the polar opposite of what otaku who like natural-looking Lolitas look for in a girl.

★**Who's at fault?:** When Keiko went to the beach with the Genshiken members, she bumped into her current boyfriend.

★**Looks are important:** Right after Keiko told her brother that she can't stand ugly guys, she saw Kousaka and proved her point by falling in love with him on the spot.

Keiko Sasahara

★**Forbidden love:** After Kousaka saved her from her violent boyfriend, Keiko fell even more seriously in love with him. But Kasukabe would have none of it.

I REALLY AM FALLING FOR HIM.

OH, NO...

SO...

THAT MEANS THERE'S A WAY I CAN BEAT KASUKABE-SAN.

★**"Kasukabe-san":** Keiko remembers to show a little respect for her rival in love.

★**Understanding:** Keiko accommodates her brother and his new stash of porno fanzines by not crashing at his place for the night. She's slowly learning how otaku operate.

I MEAN, DON'T YOU WANNA *ENJOY* ALL THE STUFF YOU BOUGHT TODAY?

RIGHT, KANJI? ♡

WELL, I GUESS IT IS IN MY BLOOD.

★**Potential:** Keiko believes that since her brother is an otaku, she has the potential to be one, too. But in general, girly girls and otaku are as different from each other as you can get.

Limited-Edition Rare Card

If an item is "rare," that means only a small number were made. In the case of trading cards, it means that very few were printed, and that they're hard to find. Cards from a first print run and cards that are exclusively available at events are called limited-edition rare cards.

Hard-core S&M

Hard-core S&M porn games are especially brutal because they involve girls who can be even younger than 10 years old. The player acts out S&M games with them, or rapes captive girls.

Tsurupeta Attributes

The "tsurupeta" referred to here points to young girl characters that have no pubic hair and have flat chests. "Blank-blank attributes" is a common term otaku use when categorizing characters. Among the famous term is "little sister attributes."

Action Figures

Action figures are made with moving parts that allow you to pose them in different positions, unlike the rigid models that are only used for display purposes. With several action figures you can re-create scenes from anime or manga.

Otaku Hideaway

"Otaku hideaway" can refer to a room that an otaku lives in, or a room that's decorated to match an otaku hobby. What kind of hideaway it is depends on whether the otaku in question is into porn or cosplay or something else entirely.

Moe Degree

There are many theories on the origin of the word "moe," but basically it is used by otaku to describe their love for a character, or to praise a characteristic, such as "girls with glasses...moe." The moe degree just describes the level of it.

CHAPTER 3

Love Within the Genshiken

THE SOCIETY FOR THE STUDY OF MODERN VISUAL CULTURE

College clubs can be rife with complicated relationships, especially when it comes to love. The Genshiken has people who look like perfect matches but have completely different personalities, and people who seem like an unlikely pair on the surface but have similar tastes and hobbies. We'll take some time to analyze the problems that come with finding love in a club, and some ways of solving them.

Problems and Solutions Part 1

Saki Kasukabe
who are total opposites

At first glance, Kousaka and Kasukabe look like a match made in heaven. But the truth is that Kasukabe is a normal person, and Kousaka, despite appearances, is a complete otaku. To illustrate what's going on here, let's think about how staff are trained at clothing stores. They're taught that the correct way to approach a customer is to say, "This is the current trend, and this one is cute. It looks great on you!" Most women react to words like "current," "trend," "cute," and "looks great on you!" But those terms can have the opposite effect on male customers.

Makoto Kousaka ♥ Saki Kasukabe

Love Among Club Membe

Makoto Kousaka

The miracle couple

I DIDN'T KNOW YOU WERE TAKING IT SO HARD.

Most men hate going along with trends, and they choose clothes based on the quality of the fabric, the label, or the uniqueness of the item, rather than by the design. Being told that something looks good on them is only background noise for men who decide whether something has value according to their own standards, rather than other people's opinions.

Starting from this assumption, we can suggest that women are more inclined to follow trends, and men lean naturally toward being otaku. In this sense, Kousaka and Kasukabe may be the ultimate couple. But they're not merely opposites; they also understand each other. Kasukabe understands that an otaku needs a night to himself after buying porn fanzines, and Kousaka can sense the changes in Kasukabe's mood and support her when she needs it.

Ordinary people who are more like Kasukabe may see Kousaka as nothing but a good-looking weirdo; likewise, otaku like Kousaka will always see Kasukabe as an alien.

But these two have overcome that obstacle and are building a relationship, and they may well be the archetypal lovers of the 21st century. We can all hope that they persevere.

Problems and Solutions Part 2
Kanako Ohno
with matching tastes

In Japanese, the term *fushou fuzui* is used to describe a perfect couple. Anyone can see that Tanaka and Ohno are perfect for each other, with Tanaka using his skill to make costumes for Ohno to wear at events. When the Genshiken went to the beach, the two of them spent time making a sandcastle together. It was a heartwarming moment.

If they do somehow run into problems together, it would probably be due to a difference of opinion about the philosophies and principles of cosplay.

Since they both have very strong feelings about cosplay, it could be difficult for them to make up after that kind of fight. But they should be fine as long as they're considerate of each other's feelings on the matter. Another thing for them to be careful of is the possibility of Tanaka getting jealous.

Souichiro Tanaka ♥ Kanako Ohno

Love Among Club Members

Souichiro Tanaka

The golden couple

Obviously, Ohno has many male fans. She looks old-fashioned and shy, but she did grow up in the United States—it's possible that she may be open about relationships.

Every time she participates in a cosplay event, there's the risk of developing obsessive fans who may go as far as stalking her. You never really know when these amateur paparazzi might attack. It's under these circumstances that Tanaka's manhood may feel threatened.

If he shoos Ohno's fans away, he'll be seen as jealous; on the other hand, he can't let them get too close, in case they turn out to be dangerous. He has to walk the fine line of protecting Ohno without showing any hint of jealousy.

Another thing to remember is that couples with perfect beginnings can only go downhill from there. These two need to work at maintaining a healthy relationship by seeking new depths in their shared hobby, cosplay.

The Tricky Relationship Between Girls Part 1

Kasukabe vs Ohno

They pick on each other a lot, but they're still friends

Kasukabe is well on her way to being a grown-up, while Ohno is physically developed but still mentally immature in some ways. That difference between them is one of the reasons why Kasukabe teases Ohno and enjoys watching her get a little bit rattled.

But Ohno doesn't always sit back and take it—sometimes she fights back with a puppy's playfulness. She relies on Kasukabe, though, and the two of them are satisfied by their relationship. It's important to remember that Kasukabe does show Ohno respect by not saddling her with a nickname like she does with the older Genshiken members. Likewise, Ohno shows good upbringing by politely calling Kasukabe "Saki-san."

In short, while their personalities and hobbies couldn't be more different, the two of them share a mutual respect and understanding.

Ohno vs Ogiue

The Tricky Relationship Between Girls Part 2

Ohno vs Ogiue

The ugly battle between two otaku

Ohno is an open otaku who can talk freely about what she likes. Because of that, she has trouble with someone like Ogiue, who refuses to be true to her otaku self. But Ogiue grew up in the Tohoku region, one of the most conservative places in Japan, and believes that girls should keep their otaku hobbies a secret. She can't stand the casual attitude that lets Ohno talk so easily about her cosplaying lifestyle.

What we have here is a pair of girl otaku who are both into yaoi, and who are worlds apart when it comes to accepting or denying that side of themselves.

They are like the north ends of two magnets, repelling each other when they're in the same room. But the day is coming when something will bring them together as close comrades.

The Tricky Relationship Between Girls Part 3

Kasukabe vs Ogiue

An older girl watches out for a younger one

Kasukabe is 20 and Ogiue is 19, but that one-year age gap makes a huge difference. Ogiue may be Ohno's archenemy, but Kasukabe—who acts like a big sister to everyone in the Genshiken—can only see her as a little girl who gets hurt easily. Kasukabe will say all kinds of things to Ogiue, but she respects her privacy (unlike, say, Kuchiki).

The feisty Ogiue doesn't take things lying down, either. When Kasukabe commented on her clothes, she went out and bought girly clothes that made Kasukabe freak out a little.

One notable thing that's come up is Kasukabe's suggestion that Ogiue might be interested in Sasahara. We still don't know if she said it to amuse herself, or if she was really picking up on Ogiue's feelings.

THE SOCIETY FOR THE STUDY OF MODERN VISUAL CULTURE

The Otaku Ten Commandments (by Madarame)

If you pay attention to Madarame, you'll learn much of the philosophy of living as an otaku. After all, Madarame's otaku spirit is very strong! Up next, we present 10 of his wise sayings.

One

When buying fanzines, do not look at the price.

HE DOESN'T LOOK AT THE PRICE.

When Madarame shops for fanzines, he makes his selection without looking at the price. No amount of stressing over money is as bad as the regret you might later feel if you pass up that special zine, so it's better to follow your gut instinct. Even if you wind up without much money to live on, you can't cut back on your fanzines! This is the basic principle of Madarame's lifestyle.

Kasukabe got worried when she found anime porn in Kousaka's room. Madarame "reassured" her by pointing out that he doesn't have a single piece of regular porn. According to his theory, anyone who can't jerk off to anime either lacks imagination or has a brain defect.

Two

I don't have a single piece of regular porn.

Three

That's the main hall over there.

SASA-HARA!

THAT'S THE MAIN HALL OVER THERE. THAT'S THE BATTLEFIELD. ONCE WE'RE IN THERE, IT'S EVERY MAN FOR HIMSELF.

That's the battle-field.

The lines to get to the main hall are long, but they're only a warm-up. The real battle—waiting in line in earnest—begins once you get into the hall. Actually buying the fanzines is only the result of that battle. Even if you collapse because you can't stand anymore, you stay in line. That is the law of Comic-Fest.

Four

Okay... I gotta do what I gotta do!

Gotta make it to God's doorstep.

Madarame broke his right hand when he slipped and fell at Comic-Fest. But he ignored the pain, even though he was sweating like crazy, because he couldn't back down from his chance at glory. After all, overcoming impossible obstacles puts you on the path to heaven.

Five

"Buy now think later!"

Sasahara wanted to buy a computer, but he didn't have the money. According to Madarame, he was thinking about it all wrong. You don't give up your dream of buying a computer just because you're broke! Instead, you buy the computer and figure out how to pay for it later. Otaku need to put their love of possessions above anything else.

When Madarame saw a hair sticking out of Kasukabe's nose, he couldn't decide whether to tell her or not. If he pretended not to notice it because he was scared of her, he would lose. Leaving the room would also mean losing. Before defeating the external enemy, he knew he needed to overcome his fear.

Six

If I don't, I'll feel like I chickened out.

Seven

He gets carried away
when he's talking
about that stuff.

Girls communicate by talking about how they feel, while guys understand each other just by exchanging information. In that sense, otaku are true men! They learn everything they can about the things they like, and can talk about those things all night. That's the mark of true otaku.

Seven/Eight

The Comic-Fest is the gathering of the biggest otaku in Japan. A healthy, tanned otaku who looks like an athlete is like a sumo wrestler who worries about his figure and goes on a diet: It's a good way to get laughed out of town. Otaku should live only for their hobbies, and arrive at Comic-Fest looking unhealthy and pale.

I'LL BE SO EMBARRASSED IF I END UP GOING TO THE COMIC-FEST WITH A TAN.

Eight

I'll be so embarrassed if I end up going to the Comic-Fest with a tan.

Nine

You don't become an otaku by trying. You just wake up one day and realize that you are one.

Kasukabe said "one of the Genshiken guys" said that, but there's no doubt it was Madarame. If you can choose to become an otaku, you should also be able to stop. But you can't help it if you just become one naturally. If you can't go back, you may as well go forward.

Ten

The air is way too thin up there for an otaku like me. I'll go crazy! I'll die from lack of oxygen.

Just as Ultraman could last for only three minutes on Earth, the fashionable stores in Shibuya and Harajuku are forbidden territory for Madarame. He has no trouble with porno fanzine shops in Akihabara, but just walking into a trendy store makes him have trouble breathing. If it gets bad enough, he passes out.

Basic Otaku Terminology Part 3

Strange Festival

The Strange Festival is a plastic model event that comes up in "Genshiken." In the real world there are events like "Wonder Festival" and "JAF-CON" that are large gatherings of otaku who love figures.

Camera Boy

Camera boys are like paparazzi in training, who can be found anywhere from cosplay photo shoots to pop idol concerts...really, anywhere they have a chance of getting a panty shot. They have professional-level equipment, and some of them have absolutely no knowledge about the characters.

Fanzine Store

These are stores that sell fanzines, fan-made software, fan-made CDs, and fan-made merchandise. A lot of doujinshi artists sell their work at fanzine events first, then have the stores carry them on consignment.

Having your own booth

In order to sell fanzines at Comiket, a group (or "circle") needs to apply in advance to reserve exhibition space. On the day of the event, they can use a circle ticket to get in early to prepare their booth.

Offset Book

Mainstream fanzines are offset books. They're not printed as clearly as illustration books, but they still look professional. Large circles that print a lot of copies of their fanzines can easily recoup the cost of offset printing.

Yaoi Book

A yaoi book is a fanzine that depicts graphic love scenes between males. The term is originally an acronym of the phrase "Yama-nashi, ochi-nashi, imi-nashi," which translates as "no climax, no punch line, no meaning."

Genshiken's Required Reading: "Kujibiki Unbalance"

THE SOCIETY FOR THE STUDY OF MODERN VISUAL CULTURE

"Kujibiki Unbalance" is a popular romantic comedy manga that inspired countless anime series and video games. It is serialized in *Monthly Shonen Magazoon*, and is a frequent topic of discussion among the Genshiken members, who based their fanzine on it. If you don't know who the president and Tokino are, you can't really call yourself an otaku.

What is "Kuji-Un"?

"Kujibiki Unbalance" ("Kuji-Un" for short) is a romantic comedy that runs in *Shonen Magazoon* (Kodansha). In addition to being the basis for games like "Unbalanced Fighter" and "Another Stories," it was the inspiration for a TV anime series. Many otaku center their fanzines or cosplay around it.

The story unfolds at Rikkyuoin High, a peculiar high school that solves all of its problems via kujibiki lottery. Even its entrance exams are determined by a lottery. The series follows several aspiring student council members over the course of a year. The main characters, Chihiro and Tokino, are popular, and so is the cool, helmet-wearing president.

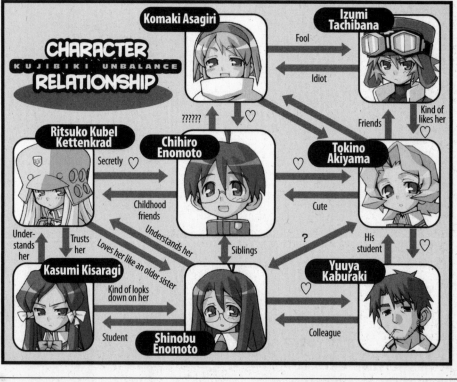

"Kuji-Un" Character Guide Izumi Tachibana / Chihiro Enomoto / Tokino Akiyama / Komaki Asagiri

Komaki Asagiri

Chihiro Enomoto

Tokino Akiyama

Chihiro, the hero of the story, is a sophomore at Rikkyuoin High. His name gives people the impression that he's a girl, and he's a candidate for the next student body secretary. On the first day of school he meets Tokino and immediately falls in love; because of that, he wants to be part of the next student council with her and Izumi. Five years ago (when he was only 10), his parents died in a car accident, and since then he and his older sister have lived alone. Unlike his sister, he's good at cooking and cleaning, so he does most of the chores around the house.

Like Tokino, Komaki is a junior and a candidate for the next student council. Komaki lives with her mother (a nurse who is never home), three rowdy little brothers, and a shy, quiet little sister. Her father was a truck driver, but he died in an accident seven years ago. At first glance Komaki looks devilish, but she's a hard worker who attends high school via a grant. She takes care of the house and her siblings, makes good grades, and makes snacks with the skill of a pastry chef. The scarf she always wears has yet to be explained.

Tokino ("Akino") is a junior at Rikkyuoin High, and the heroine of the series. She was chosen (by kujibiki lottery) as a candidate for the next student body president, and she, Izumi, and Chihiro are aiming to be the next student council. She is beautiful, talented, and friendly—and also a little mysterious. You can't exactly call her "bubbly." She has very strong intuition, which helps her to resolve different problems, but sometimes she makes things worse. She loves mushrooms, and always carries a picture book called "Mushrooms Around the World." Her weak points include tone deafness, a horrible singing voice, and a total inability to do housework.

Yuuya Kaburaki

Shinobu Enomoto

Shinobu, Chihiro's older sister, is the math teacher at Rikkyuoin High. She's also Tokino's homeroom teacher. When she wears her glasses at school, she's a serious, hard worker. But when she takes them off at home, she's bossy and lazy. She's something of an alcohol connoisseur, and especially loves Japanese sake. She has a hard time dragging herself out of bed, and spends her days off in her underwear because she's too lazy to get dressed. She's so good at switching between these personalities that she herself doesn't know who she really is.

Lisa Humvee

Yuuya [is] a biology teacher at Rikkyuoin [Hig]h, and he is Chihiro's homeroo[m te]acher. He is gruff and silent, an[d has]n't been able to open up to wor[ld] since losing his lover. People hav[e a] hard time seeing past his curtness, [but] he's a kind person with a lot of i[ntegr]ity. One small clue to his true pers[onal]ity is that he takes the time to lear[n all] of his homeroom students' names [on] the very first day of school.

Lisa is a senior at Rikkyuoin High, and serves as the current treasurer. Her parents are Americans, but she was born and raised in Japan and has dual citizenship; she loves Japanese food like sushi, soba, and natto, and despite her American blood she doesn't speak English very well. But she's a genius with the abacus, which is why Ritsuko recruited her as the treasurer. Lisa is very loyal to Ritsuko, who intervened when she was being picked on.

Kaoruko is a Rikkyuoin High sophomore, and the rival team's candidate for secretary. She is the only person who tries to intervene when Kamishakujii becomes unstoppable, but she's not very good at it. Usually she just winds up mumbling "uh... uhhh..." as Kamishakujii drags her off. She has a good figure that she can't quite hide, which also irritates Kamishakujii.

Renko Kamishakujii

Kaoruko Yamada

Mugio Rokuhara

Mugio is Chihiro's best friend and classmate. He's popular with the girls, and in junior high girls often asked Chihiro to hook them up with him. But Mugio isn't interested in having a girlfriend, and the girls spread rumors about him and Chihiro. As far as the school's tournament goes, he was disqualified early on, and is cheering for Chihiro's team.

Renko is a junior at Rikkyuoin High. She is part of a team competing against Chihiro's, and a candidate for the presidency. She and Tokino have known each other since kindergarten, and she holds a grudge against Tokino for making her wet her pants when they were small. She's the kind of person who runs into situations without thinking them through, but it's hard to hold it against her. Similarly, she reads fast enough that she can memorize a book in 10 seconds...but she forgets it again three minutes later.

CAST

Chihiro Enomoto	Yuka Imai
Tokino Akiyama	Akemi Kanda
Izumi Tachibana	Yuko Kaida
Komaki Asagiri	Yukari Tamura
Ritsuko Kubel Kettenkrad (President)	Saeko Chiba
Kasumi Kisaragi (Vice President)	Ayako Kawasumi
Lisa Humvee	Kana Ueda
Shinobu Enomoto	Haruko Momoi
Mugio Rokuhara	Kenichi Suzumura
Yuuya Kaburaki	Kazuhiko Inoue
Renko Kamishakujii	Ikue Otani
Kaoruko Yamada	Yuko Goto

くじびき
アンバランス
KUJIBIKI UNBALANCE

一綴目 「出会いはアンバランス」

©2004木尾士目・講談社／現視研究会

	SCREEN	SOUND
	#1 Part A [NOTE: this means episode 1, the first half]	
1	F.I. Follow slowly. A teddy bear is being dragged. It's a little dirty.	(SE) (Dragging sound) (BGM) C-1~13 (Whole notes, alternating discord and harmony)
2	The president (as a child) is dragging the teddy bear and walking sluggishly.	
3	The president is looking down while walking.	
4	The president is looking down while walking.	
5	(camera tilts) Looking into her face. Expression: almost crying.	
6	Fist clenched. Sleeve is a little long.	
7	She looks even more like she's going to cry. Holding it back.	
8	The president stops and looks up.	
9	Young Chihiro is standing in front of the president (can't see his face).	
10	Facing forward, looking down.	
11	Chihiro's hands clench (almost fists). [continues on page 103]	

	The president flinches. Clenched fist relaxes.	
12	Long shot. Dead trees.	
13	The president's face crumples. Tears well up. Cut right before the tears start falling.	
☆	Opening theme	
14	Looking down, wide-angle perspective. Chihiro's house. A coffeemaker giving off steam.	(SE) Glop glop glop glop... Fooosh
15	Wide-angle perspective. Toaster. Toast pops up.	(SE) Sound of heated metal (SE) BOING!
16	Wide-angle perspective. Ham and eggs in frying pan. They look delicious.	(SE) SIZZLE CRACKLE CRACKLE
17	Chihiro from behind, cooking (in apron). Turns off the heat and faces door, calling out.	Chihiro (OFF): "Nee-chan! Wake up!"
18	Places a plate of nicely made ham and eggs on the table.	(lines run over)
19	Stairs Chihiro IN (in uniform)	(SE) Footsteps Chihiro (OFF): "I'm leaving now...

KUJIBIKI

UNBALANCE

	Talking to the top of the stairs.	(stops, then says) ...try not to be late, okay?"
20	Front door. There is a false morel. Chihiro IN, talking over his shoulder.	Chihiro: "Oh, yeah—this thing in the front door...
21	Close-up of false morel. Grotesque. Looks like a brain.	(without pause) ...leave it alone! Don't put it in the fridge or something!"
22A	Stairs. Shinobu comes falling down the stairs in her underwear.	(lines run over a bit) (SE) WHUMP THUMP WHUMP THUMP
22B	Shinobu, falling down the stairs, bumps her head on the wall. Shinobu holds her head and crouches. Chihiro IN.	THUMP BONK! Shinobu: "..."
23	Looks worried but also appalled.	Chihiro: "...are you okay?"
24	Shinobu looks up. She gets mad, sounding like she has a hangover.	(line runs over a bit) Shinobu: "Yeah, yeah! I know! Leave me alone!"
25	Relieved.	
26	(camera tilt) Enomoto house. Subtitle IN.	(SE) (Door opening and closing) Chihiro: "I'm going!" (BGM IN)
27	A trash can at the gates of the train station. Trash can is overflowing. A lady throws away a magazine. The lady doesn't stop. Keeps going and OUT.	(SE) (loud noises of a train station)

KUJIBIKI UNBALANCE

	Magazine not completely in trash can. Multiple people hurrying by. (IN ~ OUT) A hand reaches for the magazine (Mugio).	
28	Mugio looks through the magazine. Looks at the other side, too.	
29	Chihiro comes running over. A little rushed.	Chihiro: "Sorry, Mugio!"
30	Mugio turns, expressionless.	(line runs over) Mugio: "There you are, you lucky thing."
31	Front of station. Chihiro runs up. He stops, out of breath.	Chihiro: "What're you talking about?"
32	Mugio shows the horoscope section. Chihiro looks at the magazine. Wry smile.	Mugio: "April's going to be your lucky month. And you're going to meet someone, it says." Chihiro: "I'm not going to count on it." Mugio: "Say what you want.
33	The trash can. The magazine is thrown away.	But the fact...
34	Gates. Chihiro topples and stops. Mugio continues to walk, then OUT.	...that this is your first day of school means that you were lucky at least once already." Chihiro: "You mean because I drew the winning kujibiki to get into this school, right? But maybe I used up all of my luck with that..." (SE) WHUMP
35	Chihiro is stuck at the gates. Mugio looks back, standing ahead.	(SE) School bell
36	Walking while looking up, going under the arch. Walking a little bit faster than normal. Entrance to Rikkyuoin High comes into view. Facing forward, PAN-UP. High-rise school buildings.	Chihiro: "I feel like my luck ran out." Mugio: "Miracles happen for people who believe in them." (pause) Chihiro: "You're not helping." (pause) Mugio: "Sorry."
37	Chihiro looking up. New students are walking behind him.	Shinobu (OFF): "New students, stand up."
38	Auditorium. New students get up from their seats.	(line runs over) (SE) WOOSH
39	At the side of the stage, Shinobu is using the microphone to give instructions. She's acting like a proper teacher. She backs away.	Shinobu: "The student body president will give a speech now."
40	Shinobu catches her foot on a cord and loses her balance.	
41	She grabs the microphone to stop her fall, but twists and falls out of the screen.	Shinobu: "!"
42	Stairs.	(SE) WHUMP THUMP WHUMP THUMP
43	Shinobu hits her head on the floor. The microphone falls, too. Major feedback.	(SE) BONK! (SE) BONK! (SE) SCREEEECH
44	New students don't know how to react.	(SE) EECH

KUJIBIKI

UNBALANCE

45	Chihiro looks embarrassed. Everyone else is expressionless.	Chihiro (whispering): "...Nee-chan..."
46	Shinobu continues as if nothing happened.	Shinobu: "The student body president will give a speech."
47	The president walks down the middle. Students in the background.	President: "Yes."
48	Chihiro looks up.	
49	Profile of president, can't make out her expression. Students in the front are blurred. IN ~ OUT	
50	Chihiro looks. Everyone but Chihiro is blurred. President IN ~ OUT blurred. Chihiro follows her with his eyes.	
51	President steps forward. Stops, pauses.	
52	Full body of the president, standing like a leader. Chest out PAN-UP	(Speak after PAN-UP) President: "Welcome to our school." (M) President's theme BGM IN
53	Front view of face.	
54	Camera tilts. Cut to chest up. But T.U. to face (layer).	
56	Layer T.U. Chihiro.	

57	Outside classroom.	Kaburaki: "Yoshida." Yoshida (male): "Here." Kaburaki: "Lancaster." Lancaster (female): "Here." Kaburaki: "Watabe."
58	Writes name on board. Kaburaki is standing, attendance book in hand.	Watabe: "Here." Kaburaki: "Everyone's here, eh? Well, I guess no one would skip school the first day.
59	Full view of classroom. Kaburaki walks toward the door. A serious student raises his hand and stands up.	There will be an announcement from the student body soon. Until then, do what you want. See you!" Student A: "Shouldn't we introduce ourselves?"
60	Kaburaki speaks with no expression. Starts walking again.	Kaburaki: "Do it on your own. You're old enough. You don't need instructions."
61	Students look unhappy with Kaburaki as they watch him leave. Mugio stands up. Chihiro looks on.	Student A: "What the heck? He's such a slacker." Students: "(appalled noises)" Student B: "Well, that's a great start to the year..."
62	Wide angle, yard. Cherry trees in bloom. Mugio and Chihiro are there.	Mugio: "I think he's a hit." Chihiro: "Huh?" Mugio: "Our homeroom teacher." Chihiro: "Oh, yeah."
63	Mugio looks at blossoms, Chihiro sits with his legs crossed. Cherry blossoms fall. Chihiro looks up at blossoms. Mugio continues, eyes still on blossoms.	Chihiro: "He knew our names without looking at the attendance book." Mugio: "Yeah." Chihiro: "Everyone probably just wants to believe in their luck." Mugio: "You talk like it doesn't involve you."
64	Cherry blossom trees that Chihiro's looking at.	Chihiro: "Yeah...I think I'm lucky just to be at this school. I can't ask for more."
65	Mugio looks at Chihiro. Chihiro notices, with a wry smile.	Mugio: "What're you saying, lucky boy?" Chihiro: "Don't call me that. Oh!" Mugio: "Huh?"
66	Chihiro stands up.	Chihiro: "I have to look something up."
67	Library (a large one). PAN-DOWN Chihiro is looking for a book.	(SE) Sound indicating large space.
68	Pulls out an old book that says "Mushroom Encyclopedia." It's as fat as an *Afternoon* magazine.	Chihiro: "I wish she would stop...
69	Camera follows Tokino walking.	...buying weird things.
70	Looks through "Mushroom Encyclopedia."	I wonder where she found that, anyway?
71	Bookshelf in back is blurred. Can't find what he's looking for. Hears a voice. Looks up.	I don't think she went out and picked it herself. Not even Nee-chan would... Let's see, it's ugly, brown, and wrinkly, and..." Tokino: "...it has a reddish top." Chihiro: "?!"
72	Closes eyes and speaks as if she's reading a description.	Tokino: "Its shape is like an irregular sphere.

	Tokino raises her head slowly.	The stalk is soft and white, almost a cylinder. In springtime they grow in conifer forests.
73	Chihiro looks on, dazed.	They grow from five to...
74	Tokino is hugging a book about mushrooms. She walks toward Chihiro slowly.	...eight centimeters. At times, large ones can grow as tall as 15 centimeters.
75	Tokino.	...they are poisonous."
76	Chihiro is mesmerized by her.	Chihiro: "..."
77	Tokino turns and sits on the table, flipping through the mushroom book.	Tokino: "But not to worry. You just have to make sure you don't inhale the steam...
78	Picture book opens up to the page on false morels.	...when you boil it.
79	A fishy look on Tokino's face. A little sexy, but dangerous.	Once boiled, it has a nice texture, like a young man's heart. When you put it in your mouth it's soft, like a rosy-cheeked maiden.
80	Tokino looks straight at Chihiro. Chihiro's heart thumps. Chihiro looks away.	The aroma is as subtle as the lands gods live in..." Chihiro: "!" Tokino: "Mushrooms are fungi, did you know?" Chihiro: "Uh, yes."
81	Wide-angle perspective. Chihiro can't move.	Tokino: "Spores bud and become bacterial thread, then the bacterial threads combine and become a germ, and the germ grows to become a mushroom.
82	Tokino with tears welling up in her eyes. She blinks, and tears fall.	Simple but strong. They grow without hesitation. Truly a higher organism...that is the mushroom. Do you understand?"
83	Tokino's face comes close enough to kiss.	Chihiro: "Yes..." Tokino: "Don't you just love them?" Chihiro: "!
84	Chihiro's heart is thumping fast.	Well...love, that's..."
85	Glasses fogged.	Tokino: "..."
86	Entire face.	Chihiro: "Yes, I love them."
87	Tokino nods with a bright smile.	Tokino: "Good!"
88	Tokino leaves, twirling her skirt as she turns.	Tokino: "Please don't forget that feeling. Then the mushroom will become your friend, master, and spouse. It will always be by your side. Your meeting is destiny." (SE) CLOP CLOP (footsteps)
89	Chihiro alone in the library.	
90	No sign of Tokino.	
91	In a daze.	Chihiro: "...Destiny..." (SE) School P.A. jingle
92	(Classroom) Chihiro sitting at desk. Shallow T.B.	Vice President (through PA system): "All sophomores and juniors, this is the student council. We are holding the first kujibiki lottery, so please proceed to the auditorium."
93	A heavy Duralumin case is set down.	(SE) THUD!
94	Auditorium. Cut at the beginning. SP. A little movement.	Vice President: "Everyone, I'm sure you're aware of this...

"Kuji-Un" Anime Script

95	The vice president adjusts the microphone. In the back is the president, looking stern.	...but we will do the kujibiki lottery now. Please take one lot each.
96	The Duralumin case is set aside. When opened, there are triangular lots inside.	The number and writing on your lot will determine which position you will fight for, and who your allies are."
97	Students line up and draw lots, one by one.	
98	Chihiro in line. The line in the back is moving in the opposite direction.	
99	Chihiro can't forget about Tokino. The line moves. Chihiro walks on without thinking.	
100	Has the look of one in love. Comes to.	Chihiro: "...Destiny..." Chihiro: "!" [bottom] Vice President: "Excuse me...excuse me!"
101	Grabs a lot.	Vice President: "It's your turn!" Chihiro: "Oh, sorry!"
102	Multiple blurs of Chihiro. President glances at Chihiro, who goes OUT.	
105	Somebody's hand (female). Pulling out a lot.	Students: "(murmuring, either talking to each other or talking to themselves)"
106	Somebody's hand (male). Pulling out a lot.	
107	Students holding lots and talking.	
108	Chihiro opens up his lot.	

KUJIBIKI

UNBALANCE

109	"027. Secretary / cooking room."	
110	Chihiro looks at Mugio's lot and is disappointed.	(murmuring continues) Chihiro: "We're separated..." Mugio: "What, are you lonely?" Chihiro: "Of course. You're the only person I know here."
	Mugio speaks coolly, like a cyborg.	Mugio: "Just think, this is your chance to meet that one special person." Chihiro: (at the same time as the vice president) "That nonsense again?"
	The people in back go OUT sporadically.	Vice President (on microphone): "Once you get your lot, please go to the indicated place." Mugio: "Good luck, lucky boy."
	Chihiro starts getting louder.	Chihiro (at the same time as the vice president): "I told you to drop it." Vice president (on microphone): "Please go quietly and quickly."
	Mugio gives a thumbs-up. Chihiro also gives a thumbs-up, looking a little worried.	Chihiro: "..."
111	The president, Chihiro, and Mugio. Mugio walks and goes OUT. Chihiro runs and goes OUT. The president shoots Chihiro a glance.	
112	The treasurer comes by. The president looks straight forward.	Treasurer: "Did you see anyone with potential?"
113	President's clenched fist weakens.	

"Kuji-Un" Anime Script

114	Smiles a bit.	President: "...a little."
115	Treasurer laughs indifferently.	Treasurer: "Heh, then maybe this year will be more fun than I expected."
116	Chihiro runs down the hallway. He clutches his lot. He looks around. He gets flustered.	Chihiro: "(breath) Cooking room..." Vice President (on speaker): "After you get acquainted with your group, we will hold a practice match. Seniors, please be the judges." Chihiro: "Shoot!"
117	Cooking room entrance (camera tilts a bit). Chihiro IN and OUT stands in front.	Chihiro: "!"
118	Chihiro looks up and tries to go in. Tokino comes by at top speed. Chihiro flies up. Screen moves.	Chihiro: "This is the room, right?" (SE) BONK!
119	Camera tilts up until it almost sees the ceiling. Chihiro and Tokino fly up.	
120	Chihiro falls and bounces on the floor. When he bounces, the screen shakes.	
121	Twists body as he rolls.	
122	Chihiro IN. Book IN. Chihiro sees a book.	
123	"Mushrooms of the World." Chihiro's point of view.	
124	Looks frantically at who he bumped into. Chihiro PAN.	Chihiro: "!"
125	Tokino is sitting on floor, holding mouth. PAN UP. Tokino looks up. The area around her mouth is red.	Tokino: "I'm sowwy."
126	Close up on lips (sexy).	(line runs over)
127	Close up on Chihiro's cheek. T.B. Chihiro looks at where he hit. Looks at Tokino. Camera pans in to Chihiro's cheek, panicked.	Chihiro: "...oh...uh...are we in the...same room?"
128	Tokino crawls closer on all fours.	
129	Chihiro backs away.	Chihiro: "Oh, but..."
130	Tokino slides IN. Goes straight to "Mushrooms of the World." Tokino hugs book.	...are you in my..."
131	Tokino gets up immediately. Their conversation doesn't line up. Use an accent to match her movements.	Tokino: "It's okay." Chihiro: "Huh?" Tokino: "Something good will happen to you."
132	Chihiro.	Chihiro: "Um, earlier..."
133	Tokino cocks her head. Doesn't remember meeting Chihiro in the library.	Tokino: "Yes?"

134	Chihiro.	Chihiro: "Um..."
135	The door to the room opens with great force. Chihiro flinches. Izumi is standing there. Chihiro and Tokino look at her. Tokino apologizes. Izumi urges Tokino with her chin.	(SE) (Surprise) SLIDE Chihiro: "!" Izumi: "What are you doing, Tokino?" Tokino: "Sorry I was late." Izumi: "Hurry and come in."
136	Izumi looks at Chihiro. (camera tilts) Coldly.	Izumi: "Who are you?"
137	Wide angle. Chihiro is on the spot. Flustered, he digs into his pocket and shows his lot. T.U.	Chihiro: "Oh..."
138	Izumi and Tokino look. Komaki butts in.	Izumi / Tokino: "..." Komaki: "Are you in our group?"
139	Chihiro.	Chihiro: "...huh?"
140	Really wide angle on Chihiro's lot. Tokino's lot IN. Izumi, Komaki's lots IN.	
141	Tokino, Komaki, Izumi.	Tokino: "You are." Komaki: "Yup." Izumi: "Yeah."
142	Chihiro.	Chihiro: "Group?"
143	Komaki steps forward.	Komaki: "I'm Komaki Asagiri. Treasurer." Tokino: "I'm Tokino Akiyama. Um, I guess I'm the president."

KUJIBIKI

UNBALANCE

	Izumi looks diagonally up.	Izumi: "Izumi Tachibana. Vice president."
146	Izumi, indifferent.	Izumi: "And you?" Chihiro: "Oh!
147	Chihiro nervously says Bows.	Um, I'm Chihiro Enomoto! I'm the secretary! Nice to meet you!"
148	Kamishakujii's mouth, laughing loudly.	(overlaps) Kamishakujii: "Bwa ha ha ha ha ha ha ha!
149	Profile of Kamishakujii.	Ha ha ha ha ha ha ha!
150	Camera shifts on laughing Kamishakujii.	Ha ha ha ha!
151	Chihiro and group are dumbfounded. Everyone looks up slightly as Kamishakujii comes closer.	Ha ha ha ha ha ha ha ha!
152	Kamishakujii is as tall as the ceiling.	Just think, I'm up against you from the beginning, Tokino Akiyama!"
153	Tokino and group are still dumbfounded.	Kamishakujii: "Bwa ha ha ha ha!
154	Yamada and the two Suzukis are holding Kamishakujii up. Step forward and stop. Big Suzuki gets down on all fours. Kamishakujii takes a step forward.	Ha ha ha ha ha!"
155	Kamishakujii walks forward on Yamada's head. Steps down on big Suzuki's back. PAN and follow onto the floor.	
156	Jumps off. Points a finger.	Kamishakujii: "You'd better curse your destiny!"
157	Tokino thinks. Tokino asks Izumi and group. Kamishakujii throws a fit.	Tokino: "Umm? Is she in our group?" Kamishakujii: "I'm Kamishakujii!
158	Kamishakujii rattles on. Brags. She speaks of her ruined past.	Renko Kamishakujii! We went on a field trip in kindergarten! And you went to the bathroom with the teacher and took your sweet time about it! Until then I was the best in everything! I could recite my address and write my name in kanji, and I was the best at addition! But because you took your time and didn't...
159	Tokino remembers.	...come out of the bathroom...!" Tokino: "Oh, Renko-chan who wet her pants!"
160	Kamishakujii loses it.	Kamishakujii: "Aarrrgggghhh
161	Gets violent, then falls back. Yamada IN. Yamada catches Kamishakujii. Kamishakujii faints.	gghhhhh!!!" Yamada: "Oh."
162	Sexy Kamishakujii. Suddenly opens eyes. Kamishakujii yells. Punches Yamada's stomach.	Yamada: "Kamishakujii-san." Kamishakujii: "Yamada!" Yamada: "Y-yes."

	Yamada flies back.	Kamishakujii: "I told you...
163	Yamada sort of IN. Yamada falls to the floor. Can see Kamishakujii and Chihiro and gang. Kamishakujii still has clenched fists.	...not to call me '–san'! 'Renko-sama'! Call me 'Renko-sama'! And don't touch me! Your chest is really gross!" Yamada: "I'm sorry, Renko-sama."
164	Kamishakujii turns back and looks at Tokino. Points finger again. Says it again (cooler than last time).	Kamishakujii: "I will never forgive you! I'll send you to the depths of hell!"
165	Tokino thinks. Tokino grips Kamishakujii's finger.	Tokino: "Umm...okay. Let's both do our best."
166	Kamishakujii blushes. Loses it again. About to faint.	Kamishakujii: "D-d-d-don't make fun of me!"
167	Inside cooking room. President, vice president, and treasurer are standing. Follow and PAN.	Vice President: "Please hurry and come in."
168	Everyone looks. Kamishakujii has a spirited expression.	Kamishakujii: "?!"
	#1 Part A FIN	

KUJIBIKI

UNBALANCE

CHAPTER 0

The 1987 issue of "Mebaetame" and the Days of Fanzine Glory

The Genshiken has existed since before 1987. The proof? A club newsletter from that year, discovered at the back of a locker. It's a relic from the days when fanzine events were becoming popular. As a special feature, we bring you an interview with a guest who was a club member at his college, and who is very familiar with Comiket.

OH...IT WAS EVEN CALLED "MEBAETAME" BACK THEN.

I THOUGHT THEY NAMED IT THAT AFTER IT STARTED GETTING MORE PORNO-GRAPHIC.

MEBAETAME

MEBAETAME

HERE'S A BOX OF OLD MAGS PUT OUT BY THE GENSHI-KEN.

▲ They found this 1987 issue of "Mebaetame" when they were cleaning the clubroom. The picture is from an anime that was popular in 1985.

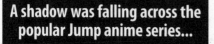

A shadow was falling across the popular Jump anime series...

This was right around the time when the anime boom was starting to die down. But anime based on manga like "Dragon Ball," "Maison Ikkoku," and "Saint Seiya" were still maintaining high ratings, and "City Hunter" and "Kimagure Orange Road" were just getting started. "Shonen Jump" manga titles were the order of the day. "Mobile Suit Z Gundam" and "Mobile Suit Gundam ZZ," which had started in the spring of 1985, came to an end in 1987. The popularity of the original series was never matched, but there was a steady influx of new fans. The giant robot boom led to the making of shows like "Metal Armor Dragonar." Meanwhile, magical girl anime like "Magical Angel Creamy Mami" were also slowing down. However, direct-to-video series were on the upswing, particularly with "beautiful girl" titles. As for video games, the masterpiece "Dragon Quest II" was released around this time, and it sold 2,400,000 units. Long lineups for buying games were becoming an issue, but girly video games had yet to find a foothold among fans. In 1987, anime was the heart of modern visual culture.

▲ Everything about the first president is a mystery—no one knows his age, or even his name. He turns up in unexpected places, and knows everything there is to know about the school.

The discovery of a 17-year-old issue of "Mebaetame."

A look back at 1987

The discovery of a 17-year-old issue of "Mebaetame."

Mebaetame

メバエタメ

1987 春号

現代視覚文化研究会

Society for the Study of Modern Visual Culture

Spring 1987 issue

Let's talk about the beautiful girls who are the highlight of the golden '80s

Beautiful girls are common these days, but it all started with Kaira-san's bathing scene in "Gangaru." Was that the very best fan service Hinno-san had to offer? It was all anyone talked about. Speaking of topless girls, that look at Romu-san's chest in the first episode was stunning. But I think she was only attractive while Studio Circus was working on the show. I know opinions vary on this issue, but that's mine.

Anyway, right now I'm more into Hana from "Dirty Twins." It's sci-fi, but their costumes reveal so much! Is that an inside joke at Sunset?

Romu or Q-ko-san? That is the question

It's clichéd to say time flies, but it's true! Only a year ago, as I was preparing to say goodbye to Romu, I promised her that I wouldn't fall for another woman. But maybe I'm getting old. I don't feel anything when I look

at the Romu-chan figurine; instead, I can't stop thinking about Q-ko-san from "Ikkoku Hall." Even the fact that she's a widow turns me on! I guess my springtime has finally come. When I close my eyes, all I hear is her kind voice... yeah, like I said, I'm getting old.

The discovery of a 17-year-old issue of "Mebaetame."

The Pros and Cons of "Cream Pumpkin"

This is my first time writing a column, and what I'm wondering is, can you honestly masturbate to "Cream Pumpkin"? I thought our priority was developing our imagination and making it more vivid. If we accept this, then we're no different from normal people who watch live action (or even the real thing)!

At first I was seduced by how sweet the combination of "anime" and "adult" sounded, but now I regret it. Hasn't our imagination reached the point where we don't need to rely on something tangible?

Onii-chan...

Classic lines from anime

Ta-dah! It's time to hand out the first classic lines award. The new face award obviously goes to Shikaru-chan from "Kimamani Lemon Road," who stole our hearts when we first heard her sweet voice saying, "Sempai?" And the classic line winner is Buru, for saying "Onii-chan" in "Gangaru Double." Something about that simple line just grabs Lolita lovers. And now, the grand winner is... Whoa, the president just smacked me and told me to nominate more lines. Sheesh, and my own father never even hit me... (to be continued).

★ A message from the president ★

We're all grateful for the chance to put out this Spring 1987 issue of "Mebaetame." I felt that the recent popularity of anime and the untapped potential of video games called for a club dedicated to studying these two aspects of modern Japanese visual culture, and so The Society for the Study of Modern Visual Culture was born! Right now anime and manga are the dominant art forms, but I think it's just a matter of time before video games or other media score a major hit. I'm interested to see how that happens.

The era of direct-to-video

Citizens, lend me your ears! Have you noticed that masturbation-worthy shows are disappearing? This suppression of beautiful girl characters will affect the future of all otaku, so we have to tackle this issue. And yet there are amazingly gorgeous girls in direct-to-video shows. Think about "Spartan X-ko," one of the gutsy sports fantasy anime that started appearing after the Hanshin won the Japan Series two years ago. Maybe TV isn't the wave of the future for anime series... (just kill me now.)

Bass is the best!

How to Get the Most Out of *Comiket*

Ken Akamatsu, the creator of "Love Hina" and "Magister Negi Magi," had a college life very much like the "Genshiken" characters'. He was part of the manga club, and an enthusiastic Comiket participant. We asked him to explain Comiket's appeal, and to tell us what it was like.

Five Rules for Enjoying Comiket:
- Newbies should go with a more experienced attendee
- Newbies should start by checking out larger circles to increase their chances of getting a good fanzine!
- Your odds of getting a good zine also go up if you choose by artist instead of by content
- It's more fun in a group
- Too much profit can spell the end of your group

Ken Akamatsu Interview

Interviewer: I hear that you've been participating in Comiket since your years at Chuo University. How did you get involved?

Akamatsu: "When I was in college I was in the manga club, the anime club, and the movie club. [note 1] At the time, 'Sailor Moon' was at the height of its popularity. [note 2] I was caught up in the wave—seriously, I heard the splash when I got hooked. (laughs) I never actually drew any manga until I started college, so I never went to Comiket before then. But after I got hooked on 'Sailor Moon,' I started making fanzines based on it."

Interviewer: What events were you participating in then?

Akamatsu: "At that point I was going to Comic City, which was held in Harumi [note 3], and Comic Revolution, which was held in Ikebukuro Sunshine City [note 4], as part of a club. This was right before 'A.I Love You' started, when I received the rookie award from *Magazine*. I was participating in fanzine events twice a month."

Interviewer: Your life really was a lot like the "Genshiken" characters', wasn't it? Having had those experiences, how do you see "Genshiken"?

Akamatsu: "It's so real, I have to wonder when Kio-sensei visited my college. You know the scene where Sasahara first joins the Genshiken and the older members trick him? [note 5] When I was a student, the building where all the clubs were was shaped like a U, and you could see into some clubs' rooms from other rooms. The movie club was on the second floor, and the manga and anime clubs were on the fourth floor, so you could look down from the anime club to see if there was anyone in the movie club room. These days there's a monorail running through the campus, and that building has been renovated, but back then I always used to buy cup noodles from the vending machine on the first floor. (laughs) [continued on next page]

Ken Akamatsu's campus life was exactly like "Genshiken"

Ken Akamatsu Interview

Note 1
Akamatsu-sensei started at Chuo University in 1988, after failing to get in when he first applied. He was in three clubs. In "Genshiken," the club newsletter, "Mebaetame," existed as far back as 1987. It lines up almost perfectly with Akamatsu-sensei's college years.

Note 2
"Sailor Moon" is a smash hit TV anime series that created a lot of beautiful-girl fans.

Note 3
Comic City is one of the biggest fanzine events in Japan. Others include HARU Comic City, held in the spring, and Super Comic City, held in May.

Note 4
A fanzine event that includes all genres, held twice a year in spring and fall. It's called C-Revo for short.

Note 5
When Sasahara was left alone in the Genshiken room, he looked under the skirts of some figurines and flipped through porno fanzines. The whole time, the club was watching him from another clubroom. (See chapter 1 for details.)

Fanzine trouble-makers like Haraguchi really exist!

So the manga feels very true to life for me. And the conversations the members had while they decided what to include in their fanzine were so accurate it's amazing."

Interviewer: "Genshiken" has some very unique characters. Do you think they really reflect people who join manga clubs?

Akamatsu: "There really are fanzine troublemakers [note 6] like Haraguchi [note 7] out there. (laughs) I don't know why, but they really do know professional artists. They have excellent connections, so they can give us information and invite us to get-togethers. Now, they themselves can't draw, and they don't have any money. But if they ask various artists to each draw just a little, they can make a fanzine. They sell that and can make up to 1,000,000 yen in just one day at Comiket. In reality, these guys are usually fat like Haraguchi. (laughs) And the president is very realistic, too—he's very smart, but he's an otaku, so he's not very popular with girls. (laughs)"
[continued on next page]

Note 6
People who try to feed off others. They prowl around the fanzine world.

Note 7
He is a member of both the Genshiken and the manga club, but he hardly participates in the former. You can see how horrible his personality is in chapter 5.

Ken Akamatsu Interview

Interviewer: How about Sasahara? He seems to want to play porno games a lot. (laughs)

Akamatsu: "I can understand how he feels. When you head off to college, you want to experience freedom, and he's still young. (laughs) Now, this is a little off-topic, and the Internet's changed things a lot, but we used to say that 'the newest images are in porno games.' I haven't played them much myself, though, other than to do a little research for 'A.I Love You.' If you try to master them, they can eat up weeks of your time, and that's just too much time to spend. But I do buy game-related illustration books for reference."

Interviewer: How about the women in "Genshiken"? Characters like Kasukabe-san, Ohno-san, and Ogiue-san are pretty unique, too.

Akamatsu: "Hmm, I wonder. I personally like Ohno-san the best. I really like that she has a lot of hair. (laughs) Speaking of cosplaying, if there is a hot girl with a miniskirt at Comiket, swarms of camera boys surround her. (laughs) [note 8] But I think the most memorable scene was seeing Kasukabe-san cry when she felt guilty about the fire. I know it's ridiculous, but as a guy, it makes me feel like, 'I have to be the one to scold her for her own good.' (laughs)"

[continued on next page]

[continued on next page]

Ken Akamatsu Interview

Note 8
Camera boys are amateur photographers who are only interested in photographing girls (and taking occasional panty shots).

Interviewer: Since you mentioned Comiket, I'd like to ask about it. When you were participating, what sorts of things were you drawing?

Akamatsu: "Well, 'Sailor Moon,' as I mentioned, but I also drew 'Sakura' [note 9] and 'Eva' [note 10]. And our manga club did release a few newsletters. We took manga that we'd submitted to *Shonen Magazine* or *Shonen Sunday*, and split them into eight parts and called them series. They were just photocopied prints, so I don't know if you could call them a magazine. (laughs) I think they're probably still in storage somewhere in the clubroom at Chuo U. I do sometimes get mail from current students, saying that they've found my old work."

Interviewer: You were pretty active, unlike the "Genshiken" characters in the first half of the series. If I had a chance, I'd definitely like to see your work from back then. By the way, how do you decide how much to charge for a fanzine?

Akamatsu: "It really depends on the generosity of the person participating. For example, let's say there's a fanzine with a color cover. We could take it and see if it's worth about 700 yen, or we might decide [continued on next page]

Large circles can make up to 10,000,000 yen in one day!

Note 9
"Card Captor Sakura." This anime was based on a CLAMP series, and became very popular.

Note 10
Aired in 1995, "Neon Genesis Evangelion" was a huge hit because of its original world-building and complex characters. It was directed by Hideaki Anno.

Ken Akamatsu Interview

that fans would pay 1,000 yen for it. If we could sell 5,000 units in one day, and we charge 200 yen, we would have a profit margin of 4,000,000 yen, including the printing cost."

Interviewer: That's a fair bit of money. I hear that the fanzines your circle releases always make record-breaking sales. For large circles, how much profit would you say they make in a day?

Akamatsu: "A typical large circle might sell about 15,000 units in a day. Usually a circle could only sell 5 units per person, but let's say they have a new fanzine for 1,000 yen a copy, and 4,000 people line up to buy it. They should be able to sell 15,000 units. If you say the cost to print each book is 500 yen, then that day's profit would be 10,000,000 yen. You also need to remember that if there are that many people in line, there's no way the circle can reach them all if everyone stops to look through the zine. So they pass out samples to the people at the front of the line, and they set the price at 1,000 yen so they don't have to spend as much time dealing with change. With 4,000 people to deal with, you lose a lot of time if you set the price at 800 yen and then have to keep giving back 200 yen in change. The customers understand the situation, so no one really complains."

Interviewer: So the circle makes 45,000,000 yen during Comiket! That's a lot of money to handle. [continued on next page]

Akamatsu: "In my experience, if you don't get bookstores to carry your fanzines, the most you could sell in a day at Comiket is 20,000 units. So if you sell the zine for 2,000 yen, your sales are 40,000,000 yen. But after the hall closes, you only have 30 minutes to count your money. A person could realistically only count about 3,000,000 yen by then, so we don't really know how much we made (laughs) when we pack up and drive home. Basically, we only have to report the income for taxes after we cross the 2,000,000 yen line."

Interviewer: I would love to have an experience like that. (laughs) Since popularity obviously affects sales, the competition at Comiket must be tough.

Akamatsu: "The different treatment is obvious, too. At every event the staff checks how long your lines are, and if they think the line is long enough, they put you near the entrance, along a wall [note 11]. If they think your popularity's dropped, they might just place you along a wall, or you might wind up on an island [note 12]."

Hint for college fanzine circles: Don't keep extra money around!

Note 11
The more popular a circle is, the closer they're placed to the wall near the entrance.

Note 12
This refers to booths that are grouped together at an event. Less popular circles are set up this way.

Ken Akamatsu Interview

Interviewer: There is fierce competition whether you're a working adult or a college student. I'm sorry to ask so many questions about money (laughs), but I would think it's hard for students to deal with.

Akamatsu: "That's true. That's why the money earned at an event should be used like this: first, subtract the printing costs, and set aside the printing cost for the next fanzine. Then use the rest of the money for the after-party, or to buy fanzines that the whole group enjoys. That way there's no extra money lying around. The thing is, money is so often the cause of a falling-out. In most cases, it's just one or two artists who're actually bringing the money in, and if they leave, the group will have a hard time surviving."

Interviewer: Money really is the source of all evil, isn't it—Comiket or no Comiket? While we're on the subject, how is the money divided among the booth staff?

Akamatsu: "Basically, the artists get the most. The editors and the booth staff [note 13] don't draw, so they don't get paid; or if they do, they would only take 10,000 yen. Or else the money would just all go to the after-party. If you're all students, everyone helps out with selling at the booth, anyway. But in a fanzine, editors like Sasahara are very

Ken Akamatsu Interview

Note 13
Staff who sell the fanzines.

important. People don't meet their deadlines if there's no one to push them. (laughs) So it's usually the most trusted person who becomes the editor."

Interviewer: Since everyone's working so hard to reach the same goal, maybe they don't worry too much about the money side of things?

Akamatsu: "Comiket starts at 10:00 A.M., and while you wait for it to start, you can feel the sense of elation filling the hall. And when they finally announce, 'Comic Market will now start,' everyone applauds and there's a huge rush of people. It's a frenzy, and time just flies. By about 4:00 P.M. you're feeling this huge sense of accomplishment, like 'It's done. Let's go drink.' Maybe I keep participating because I love that feeling."

Interviewer: Comiket started in the late 1970s [note 14]. Twenty-odd years later, have you noticed any changes?

Akamatsu: "Comiket used to be a place for young, aspiring artists to test themselves and their style. You could see how many people would line up to buy

If it weren't for Comiket, I wouldn't be where I am.

Note 14
The largest fanzine exhibition and sales event, Comic Market, started in 1978. Comiket's history goes back over 25 years!

Ken Akamatsu Interview

your product, and that became both a status symbol and a way to see how popular you were. But now that we have the Internet, that's where the young artists announce what they're doing, whether it's a job offer from a game company or being asked to illustrate a book cover. Those are the new status symbols. Lately, the trend is that they want to illustrate for light novels. Unfortunately, not that many people want to become manga artists.

On a personal note, ever since I started drawing manga for major magazines, and was given a booth position near the entrance, I've participated in Comiket as a way to connect with fans. I only sell storyboards or character portfolios [note 15], and I don't draw anything new. I charge 100 yen. I can't draw fanzines that would affect the magazine that gives me work."

Interviewer: As we wrap up, do you have any advice for people who would want to give Comiket a try?

Akamatsu: "For their first visit, beginners should go with someone who is familiar with Comiket, and line up for the major circles. Major circles rarely have bad fanzines. After that, you should look through the catalog and check out the genre you like. You might want to choose by artist rather than content.

For people who want to participate in Comiket...like I said before, I never drew manga at all until I started college. So during my student days I had a strong desire to be better at it than anyone else. Comiket helped me improve. If I hadn't participated, I probably wouldn't be here today."

Ken Akamatsu Interview

Note 15
Akamatsu-sensei is holding what he sold at last year's and this year's Comiket (character portfolios and other information). They contain illustrations you can't see anywhere else, so at 100 yen they're truly a treat for the fans.

Related information
The *Negima!* manga is available from Del Rey, wherever books and comics are sold.

Quiz: How Otaku Are You?

Read the questions below carefully and circle the answer that best describes you. Once you finish answering all of the questions, tally the points using the chart on page 132. You can see how much of an otaku you are.

Q8 Time to choose a cell phone ringtone. Which of these three options do you pick?
B The newest anime song **B** A nostalgic anime song **C** Your favorite anime song of all time

Q1 Do you often find yourself quoting lines from anime and manga in your daily life?
A Never, or I don't know **B** Once in a while **C** Not only do I say them, I act them out

Q9 The game you've been waiting for is finally going to be on sale. But there is a long line at the store. You think it might sell out before you get it, even if you line up. What do you do?
A I don't want to line up, so I'll give up **B** I'll check out the line first **C** Of course I'm lining up

Q2 Have you attended a fanzine event such as Comiket?
A Never **B** I've attended Summer Comiket or Winter Comiket **C** I participated as a circle / group

Q10 Did you understand what Madarame was talking about when he explained Ohno-san's "gufu" in chapter 13?
A I don't get it at all **B** I think I get it **C** I completely empathized with Ohno-san

Q3 You find yourself having to cosplay. What do you do?
A Wear only one item, such as cat ears **B** Gather up the courage to really go for it **C** I'm serious enough that I want to make my own costume

Q11 What comes to your mind when you think about summer and fall?
A Resorts **B** Long vacation **C** Summer Comiket and Winter Comiket

Q4 When buying fanzines, do you have a method for choosing them?
A I don't buy anything outside of my genre **B** Quantity over quality **C** I choose carefully according to the content

Q12 Do you have a type of female / male character you like?
A I have no interest in two-dimensional characters **B** Sort of, yes **C** I can tell you what kind of traits I like

Q5 If you're strapped for cash, what are your rules about financing your otaku hobbies?
A Endure not buying anything for a while **B** Think about how I can lower my cost of living **C** I'll worry about it after I buy

Q13 A computer is necessary for an otaku. What do you take into account when buying one?
A Design is important, because it is going into my room **B** Processor power **C** Whether it meets the requirements for playing porn games

Q6 Your favorite manga is going to be animated! What comes to your mind first?
A When it's going to air **B** I think about which voice actors I would choose **C** There is no way video could beat the original, so I won't watch

Q14 You find a fanzine you like at an event. How many copies do you buy, including the one you're going to keep in mint condition?
A 1 **B** 2 **C** 3

Q7 The people around you call you an "otaku." How do you react?
A I completely deny it **B** I don't have the courage to admit it **C** I know I am, so I admit it

Quiz: How Otaku Are You?

Q23 Can you identify voice actors just from hearing their voices?
A I can only tell if it's male or female **B** I know the famous ones **C** I could even name other characters the actor voiced

Q24 Can you name any scene or panel of your favorite anime or manga?
A No way **B** I could say which episode it is **C** I can say which episode and which scene (or panel)

Q25 What do you think of when you hear "Gundam"?
A I don't know it **B** Robot anime **C** I do not approve of referring to anything other than the original as "Gundam"

Q26 If you were to join a college club, which of these three would you choose?
A Manga club **B** Anime club **C** The Genshiken

Q27 Can you say the full names of all seven main characters in "Genshiken"?
A I can't even say half **B** Maybe just their last names **C** I can name them perfectly

Q28 What is the most essential trait for an otaku?
A Selective and deep knowledge **B** Futile effort **C** The guts to admit you're an otaku

Q29 How much do you spend on manga or anime merchandise, including fanzines?
A Less than 25% of my income **B** Around 50% of my income **C** More than 75% of my income

Q30 If there is an argument among your group or club, do you tend to have an entirely different interpretation of the situation and confuse your peers?
A Never had that happen **B** Maybe if I use a triple-tiered approach **C** That's my specialty

Q15 What if you could only have a meeting about just one anime series?
A No way **B** I am interested but I probably won't do much talking **C** I can stick to talking about the characters if I have to

Q16 You're about to play a fight game with your friend. How do you choose which character to play?
A I'm indecisive, so I choose a strong-looking character **B** The character I always play with **C** I can play with any character and win

Q17 Do you have a favorite line from an anime or manga?
A Not really **B** Yes **C** The line actually belongs to me now

Q18 What comes to your mind when you hear "porno____"?
A Magazine **B** Video **C** Game

Q19 Have you been to the otaku sanctuary, Akihabara?
A No **B** Yes **C** I would like to go

Q20 Which otaku type can you not stand?
A Johnny's otaku **B** Girl otaku **C** Hard-core S&M otaku

Q21 Do you understand the references made by the "Genshiken" characters?
A I didn't think they were referring to anything outside the series **B** Maybe about half of them **C** Almost perfectly

Q22 When you say "anime," which syllable do you place the accent on?
A "a" **B** "ni" **C** There is no accent

Check which answer you circled and tally up the points using the chart below. You can judge how much of an otaku you are by which "Genshiken" character you're like.

RESULTS

Harunobu Madarame (~100)

You are a master otaku. We have nothing more to say. Please continue to follow your destined otaku path. No one will stop you. No one can. You may be in danger of isolating yourself, but that's not a problem if you don't notice it.

Makoto Kousaka (~90)

You are truly a child of otakudom. You are like a prodigy who was born to become an otaku, and rise above the ranks of ordinary otaku. You can never become a normal person again.

Souichiro Tanaka (~80)

You are a semi-professional otaku. Your mind, skills, and body are those of an otaku, and you're the one who will nurture the next generation. You create various props and costumes with your artisan hands. It's too bad that your self-satisfaction stops you from developing further as an otaku.

Kanaka Ohno (~70)

You are a mid-range otaku. If you're up to this level, you're pretty respectable. You are open about loving characters, and cosplay gracefully. However, your straightforwardness may win you some enemies. Be careful.

Mitsunori Kugayama (~50)

You are a beginner otaku. You have some skill in drawing, but you lack the skills to become a professional manga artist. Your tendency to be overly fussy keeps you from rising to the next level. It is important to seek a little adventure sometimes.

Kanji Sasahara (~30)

You are making your debut as an otaku. However, you have the potential to rise to the top. What you need to become an otaku are confidence, courage, and the will to accept who you are. The first step is coming out and saying, "I'm an otaku!" Everything else will follow naturally.

Saki Kasukabe (5~10)

You are a normal person. However, you have the potential to change into anything, given the right trigger. You are most likely to change because of a significant other. If you become interested in an otaku, you may find yourself becoming more and more like them.

	A	B	C
Q 1	0	1	3
Q 2	0	1	3
Q 3	0	2	4
Q 4	0	1	3
Q 5	0	1	3
Q 6	0	1	3
Q 7	1	2	3
Q 8	0	1	3
Q 9	0	1	3
Q 10	0	2	3
Q 11	0	1	3
Q 12	0	1	4
Q 13	0	1	4
Q 14	1	2	4
Q 15	0	1	3
Q 16	0	1	4
Q 17	1	2	3
Q 18	0	1	3
Q 19	0	1	3
Q 20	0	2	4
Q 21	0	2	4
Q 22	1	3	0
Q 23	0	1	3
Q 24	0	1	3
Q 25	0	1	4
Q 26	1	2	3
Q 27	0	2	4
Q 28	0	1	3
Q 29	0	1	4
Q 30	0	1	3

CHAPTER 7

Unofficial Side Story
by Takashi Umemura and Yuka Minagawa

Takashi Umemura is well known for his popular novels based on games, while Yuka Minagawa is known for her body of work relating to various media, particularly mysteries and anime. These two talented authors have teamed up to create an original story using the characters from "Genshiken."

Takashi Umemura Born October 1973 Libra
Writer of several video games-turned-novels, including "Valkyrie Profile" and "Final Fantasy Crystal Chronicles." A groupie at heart, he is powerless against awesome or cute things. Sometimes he contracts a disease where he compulsively buys snacks and vending machine toys.

Yuka Minagawa Born in the Showa era Aries
Known as an editor for the "Official Encyclopedia of Mobile Suit Gundam GUNDAM OFFICIALS"; also the author of various series including "Tarot of Destiny."
Tends to get into anime in an unhealthy way. She is very sad that her "Genshiken" volume 4 bonus bookmark wasn't Madarame.

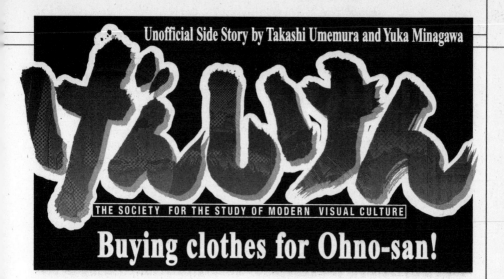

Unofficial Side Story by Takashi Umemura and Yuka Minagawa

THE SOCIETY FOR THE STUDY OF MODERN VISUAL CULTURE

Buying clothes for Ohno-san!

Tanaka-san and Ohno-san were discussing their next cosplay project, and when Ohno-san got up to get a magazine, Kasukabe-san dropped the fateful question mentioned earlier.

 [Ohno] "No, I don't."

Everyone in front of the monitor froze when they heard Ohno-san's reply. (Well, except for Kousaka-kun.)

 [Madarame] "Tanaka, is that true?"

 [Kugayama] "I-if it's true, I-I think it's a problem that Kasukabe-san knows about it."

 [Tanaka] "Um, actually... Well..."

Tanaka-san was stammering, they tell me.

Yeah, I know. His imagination was probably running away with him.

 [Kuchiki] "That must mean

 [Kasukabe] "Hey, Ohno—you don't wear pants, do you?"

From what I hear, it all started when Kasukabe-san made that one offhand comment.

It wasn't an official meeting, but just about everyone was hanging out in the Genshiken room except for me (I'm Sasahara, the current club president).

Lately all of the older club members have been so busy looking for jobs that we almost never all get together...although Madarame-san seems to be around a lot.

Anyway.

So there they all were, playing "Unbalanced Fighter" in the clubroom. Kuchiki-kun was trying to challenge Kousaka-kun. (I guess Tanaka-san wasn't really playing.)

[Tanaka] "If we want to do this character, I think we already have the material on that shelf over there."

[Ohno] "Oh, we should do it then."

GENSHIKEN OFFICIAL BOOK 134

Buying clothes for Ohno-san!

I'm ignoring you" face we've all come to know and love.

 [Kasukabe] "Ohno, where do you buy your clothes?"

[Ohno] "Tanaka-san and I have been shopping at Okabaya in Shinjuku lately."

[Kasukabe] "Okabaya?"

 [Tanaka] "You can find anything you need there, from fabric to buttons. I've heard Nishi Nippori is cheaper, but no one can beat Okabaya's fake leather selection."

[Ohno] "Why, are you finally interested in having an outfit made?"

[Tanaka] "Just give me some advance notice, and I'll make one for you anytime. We should keep the president's uni-form as a staple in your wardrobe, though."

[Kasukabe] "Yeah, right. That's not even close to what I meant."

[Ohno] "Huh?"

[Kasukabe] "I was asking about your normal clothes. You know, the ones you wear every day? That's usually what people mean when they talk about clothing."

[Ohno] "Oh. I just buy that stuff at the grocery store."

 [Kasukabe] "You've got to

that Kasukabe-sempai's been looking under Ohno-sempai's skirt! Or no, wait, it might just mean they've been doing naughty things..."

THUD!

Teaching Kuchiki-kun a lesson seems to be Kasukabe-san's role in life. She picked up the manga she'd been reading and stabbed Kuchiki-kun in the face with a corner of it. I think her temper's been making her more violent than she was when I met her.

[Madarame] "You're lucky, Kuchiki—if Kasukabe-san hadn't hit you, Tanaka probably would've strangled you."

[Kuchiki] "Ooh, I would have loved to feel Tanaka-sempai's hands on my neck. It'd probably be too much for me!"

He just never stops, does he? I heard later that he was wriggling his hips while his nose bled.

[Ogiue] "...what a filthy mind."

Even Ogiue-san, who was doo-dling in her notebook, looked up and made a face.

[Kousaka] "Are you all playing along on purpose?"

Kousaka-kun was calm as ever. Well, I guess if you think about it, Kasukabe-san wouldn't be talking about *under*pants, would she?

Kasukabe-san just kept talking, wearing the "you're all idiots and

GENSHIKEN

[Kugayama] "I-it was hanging on by a thread during winter Comic-Fest."

 [Madarame] "It couldn't keep up with your Newtype stash, eh?"

 [Sasahara] "My sister left this bag lying around, and it was the perfect size, so... Does it look weird?"

 [Kasukabe] "Well, it's not exactly *weird*, but...you only own one bag?"

 [Sasahara] "Uh, yeah."

You should've seen the face Kasukabe-san made!

She looked around the room, peering at everyone.

 [Madarame] "What is it?"

 [Kasukabe] "Do you all only have one bag?"

[Madarame] "Of course."

 [Kasukabe] "Why? You only need a small bag for everyday stuff. Why do you all have backpacks?"

When Kasukabe-san says, "you all," it doesn't include Kousaka-kun. And for the record, Tanaka-san uses a large shoulder bag, but to Kasukabe-san's way of thinking they're all the same.

[Madarame] "What are you trying to say? We're just

be kidding! If you go to a real store, there are tons of cute clothes. Why would you shop at a grocery store?"

Kasukabe-san wants to own a boutique when she graduates, so she pays a lot of attention to fashion. She was the only one who noticed when Madarame-san got new glasses the other day. (Not that he wears them anymore.)

 [Kasukabe] "Fine. I'll take you shopping. We'll call it the 'Ohno makeover project'!"

[Ohno] "Um...could you please not decide things like that on your own?"

 [Kasukabe] "Why not? There are really cute clothes out there, you know."

And that's when I walked in.

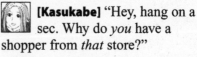 **[Sasahara]** "Hey, everyone."

[Kasukabe] "See, like that place. Although that store is mostly for girly girls, so it doesn't really match your style..."

Kasukabe-san was pointing at my bag as she explained.

[Kasukabe] "Hey, hang on a sec. Why do *you* have a shopper from *that* store?"

[Sasahara] "When I was heading out this morning, my usual bag ripped."

 [Tanaka] "So it finally went, huh?"

Buying clothes for Ohno-san!

[Kasukabe] "But it's a good bag."

[Sasahara] "Huh? But it's still only a bag. It's just for wrapping stuff in."

[Kasukabe] "Don't call it a 'bag'—call it a 'shopper.' Different words, different things."

[Kuchiki] "It's *only* a bag from a store...what a shopper!" [Note: like "shocker" if you don't get it...Kuchiki makes a BAD pun here in Japanese using the word "shopper"]

I took a close look at my "shopper" to make sure I hadn't gotten it dirty, and sighed in relief when I found it was clean. With luck, my sister wouldn't throw a fit.

[Madarame] "I can't believe you broke your backpack. What are you going to do for Evo on Sunday?"

[Sasahara] "I'll buy one before then. Or if I don't get a chance by then, I'll look for one when we get to Ikebukuro."

[Kasukabe] "What, you guys are going to Ikebukuro on Sunday?"

[Sasahara] "Uh, yes. Around the Sunshine area."

[Kasukabe] "I can't even imagine you guys there."

[Madarame] "As usual, you're too kind."

[Kasukabe] "Well, that's

girding ourselves for battle in the best possible armor. It's fine for carrying just a little bit of stuff, and it keeps both of your hands free! It's good, solid equipment! And best of all, when you have something important in it you can feel the weight of it on your shoulders."

[Kugayama] "Th-that's right. You can feel what you bought. That's pure happiness r-right there."

[Kasukabe] "...whatever. Forget it."

It's been two years since Kasukabe-san started hanging out with people like us. I guess we're getting used to each other, but at times like this you can still see the culture shock.

I still didn't really understand what she meant. When I dropped my sister's bag on the table, Kasukabe-san said,

[Kasukabe] "That bag belongs to your sister, right?"

[Sasahara] "Huh? Yeah."

Since I still didn't see what she was getting at, I must've looked confused.

[Kasukabe] "She'll probably get mad if it's in bad shape when you give it back."

[Sasahara] "Why? Isn't it just a bag you get when you shop at the store?"

GENSHIKEN

After Kugayama-san drove off, Madarame-san looked at us and said,

 [Madarame] "Okay, we should hurry, too."

 [Kasukabe] "Why are we in a hurry?"

 [Keiko] "Good question."

 [Kasukabe] "Hey, wait a minute. What are you doing here?"

 [Keiko] "Why shouldn't I be here? If everyone's shopping in Ikebukuro, I'm the obvious choice for a guide. Right, Kousaka-san?"

 [Kasukabe] "Get away from him!"

So that was one more person Kasukabe-san wasn't happy to see, but we couldn't stop to deal with it. We hurried toward the Sunshine building, where there was already a line leading to the Import Mart on the fourth floor.

 [Sasahara] "It's not as bad as Comic-Fest, but that sure is a long line, huh? Guess it's already open."

[Madarame] "People hang out by the hall even though they're not allowed to spend the night. How're they going to make up for it if the hall stops allowing us to have the event here?"

[Kasukabe] "What's this line for? What's going on?"

good enough. I'll guess I'll go, too."

I guess she was still thinking about her plan to give Ohno-san a makeover.

Back when Madarame-san bought his Akihabara outfit, Ogiue-san tried out some different clothes, too. I think maybe Kasukabe-san figured she should go shopping with Ohno-san instead of just turning her loose, like she had with Ogiue-san.

Even I knew that it wouldn't count as a makeover if Ohno-san went shopping with Tanaka-san.

So that's probably why Kasukabe-san decided to tag along on our Ikebukuro trip. Of course, if she'd known the real reason we were going there, she wouldn't have come...

Sunday.

When we planned our outing, we decided to meet up at a place where we could see the Sunshine 60 building.

 [Kugayama] "O-okay, I'll come meet up with you guys after I go park the car."

Kugayama-san had driven over with Kasukabe-san, Kousaka-kun, and Ohno-san. By the time they arrived, everyone who'd taken the train was already waiting.

[Madarame] "Hurry up."

[Kugayama] "Yeah."

Buying clothes for Ohno-san!

and the hall is much smaller than the Ariake Big Sight. It caters more to guys (maybe that's why Ogiue-san didn't come). If it weren't for Kasukabe-san's project, I don't know if Ohno-san would've turned up, either.

As we went into the hall we decided where to meet up later, and went our separate ways. We all have our favorite circles, after all.

Kasukabe-san and Keiko tagged along with Kousaka-kun, of course.

And as always, Kousaka-kun seemed oblivious to the two people following him. He went from booth to booth, not looking back even once.

That was when Kasukabe-san asked,

 [Kasukabe] "Hey, why are you scowling?"

[Keiko] "I can't believe you're okay with this."

 [Kasukabe] "Okay with what?"

[Keiko] "It reeks in here."

 [Kasukabe] "Really? Maybe it's because there are so many people."

[Keiko] "That's not it. I'm saying it reeks of otaku."

 [Kasukabe] "It's not the air in the hall?"

[Keiko] "No, it really stinks. You really can't smell it?"

I wonder if Kasukabe-san really doesn't know, or if she just asks those questions out of habit. I don't know.

 [Madarame] "It's for Evo."

[Kasukabe] "...and that's what, exactly?"

 [Sasahara] "Comic Evolution...a fanzine event."

 [Kasukabe] "Like Comic-Fest? But I thought you guys had to take the first train to get to those things."

 [Kousaka] "There was a 'Kuji-Un Only' event here last week, so today we're here to buy the ones we missed."

 [Kasukabe] "They have those every week?"

 [Kousaka] "Not every week, but that's what's going on today."

 [Kasukabe] "..."

 [Keiko] "Then maybe you should go home."

 [Kasukabe] GLARE

[Keiko] (Ooh, scary!)

So that's how Kasukabe-san wound up at Evo, even though she's so vocal about not being an otaku.

Evo is different from Comic-Fest in that it's only one day long,

GENSHIKEN

[Kasukabe] "I didn't notice because I love him."

Okay, fine.

The truth is, Kasukabe-san didn't notice because she was a smoker. That is, until she had to quit smoking after the fire incident.

Since our goal for the day was just to buy the fanzines we'd missed, it only took us about two hours to finish at Evo. So we went to the main Animebito Ikebukuro store, where we were supposed to meet up.

 [Kasukabe] "Why are we here? We're just meeting here and not shopping, right?"

 [Madarame] "It's a waste of time to be somewhere where we can only wait."

 [Kasukabe] "Why can't we go to a café?"

 [Kugayama] "B-because here, we have the option of shopping."

Kasukabe-san was surprised to see that even Keiko was looking at some anime magazines in the magazine corner.

 [Kasukabe] "Why are you looking at the stuff, too?"

Keiko was reading an ad on the back of a magazine, for "Ebisu Animation Academy."

[Keiko] "Well, I need to decide what to do after I graduate. There's nothing I particularly want to do, so I thought I

 [Kasukabe] "Umm..."

And then Kasukabe-san took a deep breath.

 [Kasukabe] "Ugh..."

The truth is, it smells.
It really does.

 [Keiko] "Monkey boy's room smells a bit, too. I guess it's the natural stink of otaku... Is Kousaka-san's room like this?"

 [Kasukabe] "You've been in Kousaka's room before."

[Keiko] "But there were other guys there, so I couldn't tell how it usually smells."

 [Kasukabe] "Kousaka's room doesn't smell."

Apparently, Kasukabe-san knew exactly what Kousaka-kun's room smelled like.

 [Kasukabe] "..."

[Keiko] "...seriously?"

[Kasukabe] ...NOD

[Keiko] "..."

[Kasukabe] "..."

The way I heard about it later, Kasukabe-san responded with,

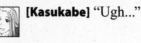

Buying clothes for Ohno-san!

But they couldn't decide on anything, so we went to the next store.

 [Kasukabe] "I think this looks good on you. Oh, but your boobs might be too big for it."

 [Ohno] (Looking down) "..."

Third store.

 [Kasukabe] "Then how about this one? No?"

 [Ohno] "No, I don't like these kinds of..."

 [Kasukabe] "Really? I think it's cute."

Fourth store.

 [Kasukabe] "This one?"

 [Ohno] "..."

 [Kasukabe] "Okay, fine. Let's go to the next one."

Fifth store.

 [Kasukabe] "Hmm, I still can't decide if this would look good. Why don't you try one on?"

 [Ohno] "Um, no. It's okay."

[Kasukabe] "...next."

Sixth store.

[Kasukabe] "Hmm, this isn't right. Let's go to the stores over there."

Seventh store.

could go to one of these otaku schools and have more in common with Kousaka-san. I do have potential."

 [Kasukabe] "...that's not an otaku training school."

 [Keiko] "Oh, really? Darn."

Ohno-san and Tanaka-san had arrived at Animebito before Kasukabe-san, and they were shopping on the other floors. When we texted to tell them that we were downstairs, they came down immediately. Kasukabe-san grabbed Ohno-san as soon as she was in sight.

 [Kasukabe] "I can't stay with these guys. I have to do what I came for. Let's go, Ohno."

[Ohno] "Huh? You really don't have to do this."

[Kasukabe] "Just come on!"

At last, Kasukabe-san was able to start spending the day the way she wanted to.

Tanaka-san followed the girls with a worried look. The rest of us followed along, too, but it was more because we were curious to see how it was going to turn out.

But going along turned out to be a bad idea, because girls' shopping is *exhausting*.

First, Kasukabe-san took Ohno-san to a store in Sunshine City.

 [Kasukabe] "Okay, let's start here."

[Kasukabe] "You're staying with us."

 [Keiko] "Ugh..."

 [Madarame] "Why does it take them so long? They're just walking in circles."

 [Kousaka] "It's always like this."

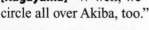 **[Kugayama]** "W-well, we circle all over Akiba, too."

[Madarame] "But sheesh. I'm about to pass out from spending so long in those normal-people stores."

 [Sasahara] "We really stuck out."

 [Kuchiki] "I'm uncomfortable in this café, too."

Because of Evo, all of the family restaurants that could hold all of us were full. So we had to resort to waiting in a Kasukabe-san-style café, sitting in a corner like we were fugitives.

Suddenly, Madarame-san grabbed his bag and held it in front of his face.

 [Madarame] "Show me Gundam! Show me the battles of Gundam!"

 [Kugayama] "H-he really is out of oxygen."

 [Kuchiki] "Maybe we should head back to Animebito."

 [Kasukabe] "Hmm... It's a little... Nah. I liked the first one."

And they came back to the first store. By this time we were completely burned out. (Except for Kousaka-kun, who was exactly the same as always.)

 [Madarame] "That's it! I can't hang around you people anymore!"

Madarame-san completely lost it right there in the store. Of course, he immediately realized that he was yelling in public and wilted in embarrassment.

 [Kasukabe] "Oh, yeah, go ahead and leave. You guys are in the way anyway. Just go wait for us at some café."

 [Madarame] "...I'll do that."

 [Tanaka] "Then I'm going to Hands."

 [Ohno] "Me too!"

[Kasukabe] "You realize the whole point is for you to be here?"

[Ohno] "Ugh..."

[Kousaka] "Then I'm going to go wait with Sempai."

[Keiko] "Oh, Kousaka-san, wait for me!"

Buying clothes for Ohno-san!

 [Madarame] "Finally done?"

Kasukabe-san shook her head.

 [Madarame] "Not yet? Not yet? How much longer are you going to take?"

[Kasukabe] "I don't know. Ask Ohno. Why are you so stubborn?"

 [Ohno] "I told you I don't need this. I don't need anything."

 [Kasukabe] "So you're saying you didn't see anything you liked, right? You didn't find anything at all you thought was cute?"

 [Ohno] "Well..."

 [Kasukabe] "You did, right? That's why I said that you should try it on."

[Ohno] "It's okay. It won't look good on me anyway."

 [Kasukabe] "That's for you to decide after you put it on and stand in front of the mirror. Why are you deciding before seeing what they look like?"

 [Ohno] "Those clothes are embarrassing."

[Kasukabe] "You wear much more embarrassing clothes when you cosplay."

[Ohno] "Cosplaying is not embarrassing!"

[Kasukabe] "Well, what do

 [Sasahara] "Are you really missing the point, or are you doing it on purpose? We're waiting for Kasukabe-san, remember?"

 [Kousaka] "Oh, here you are."

 [Madarame] "Back at last, eh? Oh—it's only you guys."

 [Tanaka] "Sigh."

 [Sasahara] "What's wrong?"

 [Tanaka] "I just went to check up on them, but..."

 [Sasahara] "What's wrong with Ohno-san?"

 [Tanaka] "I don't think she's having a very good time."

 [Madarame] "Then why don't you take her home?"

[Tanaka] "I'd just wind up paying for it later."

[Madarame] "Yeah, that's true."

[Kousaka] "That's not true. Saki-chan isn't that evil. She thinks she's doing this for a good cause."

[Tanaka] "Yeah, I'm sure she does. And Ohno-san knows that, so that's why she's going along with it."

We were still talking when Kasukabe-san and her stragglers finally arrived.

[Kasukabe] "I'm not denying it. Did I tell her that she can't dress like herself?"

 [Ohno] "..."

 [Madarame] "But..."

 [Kasukabe] "I know that she likes what she likes. I'm just asking her to consider other things, too."

 [Ohno] "..."

 [Kasukabe] "What do you think, Tanaka? Don't you want your girlfriend to look cute?"

[Tanaka] "Well, it's not like that's why I'm going out with her. Ohno-san is Ohno-san no matter what she looks like. But..."

[Kasukabe] "..."

[Ohno] "..."

[Tanaka] "But I don't like it if she's uncomfortable."

[Kasukabe] "Fine, then. I'm the only bad guy here. I'm leaving!"

And with that, Kasukabe-san walked out. It's times like this that I really admire Kousaka-san: he followed her without saying anything, and even remembered to leave money for his drink.

you mean by embarrassing? It's not that bad. It's just a little tighter than your usual clothes."

 [Ohno] "They're showy. If I wear that and walk down the street, people will stare at me."

 [Kasukabe] "No one's looking. It's not even showy! You'll get a quick reaction from guys like these and that's it."

[Ohno] "No, they'll all look. They'll look at me like I'm something strange. So I'd rather wear my usual clothes."

 [Kasukabe] "You're just self-conscious."

 [Ohno] "...!"

 [Madarame] "Hey, come on. Hold it. Let's calm down, okay?"

 [Kasukabe] "..."

 [Ohno] "..."

[Madarame] "Just let people buy whatever clothes they want."

[Kasukabe] "Then she's not going to change."

[Madarame] "You can say that all you want, but what you're doing is denying her identity. Ohno-san bases her clothes on her individuality. You shouldn't be denying that side of her."

bought a backpack just like his old one."

 [Sasahara] (Wry smile)

 [Kasukabe] "Well, it's a safe outfit, but that T-shirt isn't bad at all. It's cute."

[Ohno] "Really? Hee hee. But these 'Levisu' are pretty good."

[Kasukabe] "You pronounce that 'Levi's.' Come on, I thought you were from the States."

[Ohno] "Huh? But, uh... ummm..."

 [Madarame] "Well, we could leave Kasukabe-san to Kousaka."

I'm sure Madarame-san's heart was working overtime. Ohno-san got up as if she wanted to go after them and patch things up.

 [Ohno] "...I think I'll go shopping before I go home."

 [Tanaka] "I'll go, too."

And they were gone, leaving only an uncomfortable atmosphere for us to deal with.

 [Sasahara] "Well, I guess that just leaves us."

Of course, we knew that leaving the two girls up to Kousaka-kun and Tanaka-san was the best way to go.

 [Madarame] "Let's stop by Hebi no Ana and then head home."

[Kugayama] "Y-yeah, let's do that."

On Monday, Ohno-san looked a little different. She was wearing denim jeans and a T-shirt with a logo on it. Kasukabe-san smiled when she saw her.

 [Kasukabe] "Oh, it's good. You look great."

And Ohno-san looked like Kasukabe-san's reaction made her happy.

[Kasukabe] "You did much better than Sasa-yan did—he

Unofficial Side Story by Takashi Umemura and Yuka Minagawa

THE SOCIETY FOR THE STUDY OF MODERN VISUAL CULTURE

Buying a computer for Ogiue-san!

old enough that there weren't any toys for it anymore. Wow, those toys are really taking me back."

 [Kasukabe] "So where'd they come from?"

 [Madarame] "We had a box full of stuff we never got around to organizing. We found these inside."

 [Kasukabe] "So those are toys that the first Genshiken members bought?"

 [Madarame] "That would seem to be the case."

 [Kasukabe] "But isn't the show for kids? So those toys are for kids, right?"

I can kind of see where Kasukabe-san is coming from. When Madarame-san and I were kids, the people who were in the Genshiken then were watching the same show as we were, buying the same toys. If you think about it, it's a little weird. The sempai of that time were watching Otaru, Kanijinmaru,

 [Kasukabe] "What's that toy?"

 [Kousaka] "Ooh, Kanijin-maru!"

To no one's surprise, the couple that had just walked into the clubroom had completely different reactions to the items on the table. Kasukabe-san eyed them suspiciously, while Kousaka-san reached for them with an elated expression.

 [Kousaka] "From 'Ocean God Hero Tale Otaru'?"

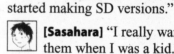 **[Tanaka]** "Yeah, this is from when easy-to-make plastic models were popular and they started making SD versions."

 [Sasahara] "I really wanted them when I was a kid."

 [Madarame] "Hmm? Wasn't it before your time? It was airing when I was still in kindergarten."

[Sasahara] "I saw it in reruns in the country, when it was

[Sasahara] "Oh. It's coming out on the same day as 'Kuji-Un' volume 7. I guess I can't buy it."

 [Kasukabe] "Huh? I don't get it. Why can't you?"

 [Sasahara] "Mostly, I just want to see it. I don't have to own it."

 [Kasukabe] "Hang on, I thought all of you guys tape this 'Kuji-Un' show."

 [Sasahara] "We do."

[Kasukabe] "Then you don't need the DVD."

[Madarame] "Tsk, tsk. You're so naïve."

[Kasukabe] "...?"

[Madarame] "Just because something comes out on DVD doesn't mean it's just what you saw on TV turned into a product. When they make DVDs, they fix the art up. There's bonus footage. In the first print run, they include original telephone cards, and when you buy the entire series they give you another special card. With all of those perks, how can you *not* buy it?"

[Kasukabe] "So you're buying the DVD for the extras. They have you wrapped around their little finger."

 [Madarame] "Urgh. No. This is an investment. An invest-

and his best friend, Sakeou, with a totally different perspective from ours.

 [Ogiue] "I watched the reruns, too. When I was in elementary school."

 [Sasahara] "Really? Did you like it?"

 [Ogiue] "Yes. That's why I went out looking for fanzines and read those—especially the ones with Otaru and Sakeou..."

Ogiue-san stopped short and turned red, looking down at the table. I guess she was watching Otaru from a different point of view, too...

 [Ohno] (Grin) "Heh."

 [Ogiue] "!"

 [Sasahara] "They don't seem to air a lot of reruns anymore."

[Madarame] "That's because these days shows get released on DVD after they air."

[Sasahara] "It's really too bad."

[Madarame] "But to make up for it, a lot of older shows are released on DVD now, too."

[Tanaka] "I think 'Otaru' is coming out on DVD soon."

Tanaka-san pulled a magazine out of his bag and pointed to the release date: the 21st of this month!

terminal. So there's no point in paying for progressive or advanced progressive technology."

 [Tanaka] "Well, that's true. Ogiue-san, does your TV have a D terminal?"

 [Ogiue] "Huh? Oh, uh... I don't really know..."

 [Tanaka] "I see. So you should make your choice according to the price and the design. It's easy if you're only going to use it to watch commercial DVDs."

 [Madarame] "Hold it. I have to step in here. In this day and age, are you truly happy with just watching? Don't you need to record, too?"

 [Kugayama] "S-so, a DVD recorder?"

 [Madarame] "Something HD, with at least 320GB, and you should be able to boost its performance by at least five times."

 [Sasahara] "So it's definitely going to be HD?"

 [Madarame] "Of course."

 [Kugayama] "But the ones that include VCRs are good, too."

 [Tanaka] "Hmm, I wonder."

 [Madarame] "It is tempting."

 [Tanaka] "Ogiue-san, is your room full of videotapes?"

ment that comes from love. The consumers support the creators and encourage them to create new series. We demonstrate it by buying their products."

 [Kuchiki] "I don't buy them. I rip them. Ripping is the best. It's the only way to get software!"

...he's such a jerk!

 [Kasukabe] "How about you, Ogiue? Do you agree with this crap about love and investments?"

[Ogiue] "I don't really follow that argument, but I do understand that you buy something you like."

[Kasukabe] "So you're going to buy that show on DVD?"

[Ogiue] "I want it, but I don't have a DVD player. I have to buy that first."

 [Madarame] "Okay, then! Let's call the first 'Le t's buy a DVD player that suits Ogiue-san' meeting to order."

[Ogiue] "...!"

[Sasahara] "There's not that much to choose between players. The prices are pretty reasonable."

[Kugayama] "Whoa, there's no love there. You need to be specific about what you want."

[Sasahara] "But my television only has a video

[Madarame] "Ah. I see, I see."

 [Tanaka] "Madarame, are you thinking..."

 [Madarame] "Well, it's just something I thought of. If you're already looking at getting a TV tuner and a DVD super multi-drive, I think a computer could do the same job."

 [Kugayama] "B-but with a computer you can't record and burn shows simultaneously."

 [Madarame] "But you have more options with it. Plus, you can play porno games."

 [Sasahara] "Ogiue-san doesn't play porno games. She's a girl."

 [Kasukabe] "She might. Ohno-san plays something like that."

 [Ohno] "Huh? Huh? Um...?"

[Ogiue] "!"

[Ohno] (Looking down) "..."

[Ogiue] "Ohno-san, you're all kinds of perverted, aren't you?"

[Ohno] "What? What do you mean? That's not true!"

[Ogiue] "You cosplay. You play porno games. You like queer old men. You're an almighty otaku girl."

 [Ogiue] "Uh, no."

 [Madarame] "So you don't need a VCR."

 [Kugayama] "Uh, so maybe a model with about 250GB?"

[Tanaka] "Sounds good."

 [Sasahara] "Actually, that's pretty luxurious."

 [Madarame] "..."

 [Sasahara] "Hmm? Madarame-san, do you have a problem with that?"

 [Madarame] "Well, it's more like I had a revelation."

[Sasahara] "Oh?"

[Madarame] "Ogiue-san. Isn't there something else you want to do?"

[Ogiue] "Huh?"

 [Madarame] "Like, something other than watching DVDs."

[Ogiue] "Uh, um..."

 [Madarame] "For example, when we were preparing for Comic-Fest, you were playing around with Photoshop. How was it? Was it fun?"

[Ogiue] "Yes...it was."

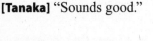

instructions on it. Unfortunately, Ogiue-san looked like she didn't understand what it said. Kasukabe-san took a peek, too.

 [Kasukabe] "Um, what does that even mean?"

Kasukabe-san clearly didn't get it either. That's why she said,

 [Kasukabe] "Okay, Sasa-yan. Go with her to get the parts."

 [Sasahara] "Huh? Me?"

 [Kasukabe] "Right. When you guys made that fanzine, you put Ogiue through a lot of trouble. So now's your chance to make it up to her."

 [Sasahara] "But that was because you—"

 [Kasukabe] "Just go."

 [Sasahara] "But I don't know much about computers..."

 [Madarame] "You don't need to worry about that. I'll make you a walking plan."

I should've clued in when Madarame-san said that, but all I could come up with was that it would be better if Madarame-san went with her.

[Madarame] "I'm busy trying to get a job."

[Sasahara] "That's not fair. You always use that as an excuse when there's work to do."

 [Ohno] "You're not that different!"

 [Ogiue] "!"

 [Kugayama] "Oh no, they're at it again."

 [Sasahara] "Although we're used to it by now."

 [Madarame] "Anyway, let's get back to the computer issue."

 [Kuchiki] "Speaking of computers, I do want a new video card."

 [Madarame] "You can rip that, too."

[Kuchiki] "Ooh, that hurt."

So our club get-together turned into a discussion about what kind of computer Ogiue-san should buy. (Although everyone else did most of the talking; Ogiue-san was just answering questions.)

"What size monitor do you want?" "How much memory do you want?" "How much hard drive space?" "What accessories?"

 [Ogiue] "Huh? Uh, um...I'm not really sure..."

Eventually we reached a decision: we'd buy all the parts and build it ourselves.

 [Madarame] "You just have to ask for the parts written here."

Madarame-san gave Ogiue-san a shopping list with very specific

Buying a computer for Ogiue-san!

 [Sasahara] (Huh? Was that my imagination?)

A guy who passed us glared at me.

 [Sasahara] (Huh? Why?)

There was another guy glaring at me from another spot in the store.

 [Sasahara] (Did I do something wrong?)

I noticed more and more people glaring at me. Finally, I looked at Ogiue-san and had a revelation. Were they glaring because I was there with a girl?

[Sasahara] (No, you guys have it wrong. Ogiue-san is not my girlfriend. She's just a kouhai. I'm just here with her to help her shop. We're not a couple. We're not on a date.)

I kept explaining myself silently to every guy who passed by.

[Sasahara] (No, it's not what you think. No, it's not what you think.)

That was when I felt someone watching me.

[Sasahara] "Huh?"

When I turned around, I didn't see anyone. But I thought I saw a familiar jacket behind a sign.

 [Sasahara] (Huh? Was that Madarame-san's Akihabara outfit?)

 [Madarame] "Besides, if you don't go, you can't make it up to Ogiue-san."

 [Sasahara] "..."

 [Ogiue] "..."

So that's how Ogiue-san and I ended up in Akihabara.

Madarame-san's instructions said to look around the computer shops to check out the market.

 [Sasahara] "I wonder if this is necessary."

 [Ogiue] "..."

 [Sasahara] "Uh, so...Ogiue-san, is this your first time in Akihabara?"

 [Ogiue] NOD

 [Sasahara] "Oh, I see. Well... let's go, then."

[Ogiue] NOD

It might have been her first time going into a store like this. Her black eyes were staring at the computers, one by one. I kind of got the feeling she wasn't doing that because she had to buy one, but because she felt it was the right thing to do.

Or maybe she didn't know what else to do.

Because she was with me.

Once that thought crossed my mind, I started to get nervous.

That's when...

[Madarame] "We can't see inside the store from here."

 [Kasukabe] "Whoa, what is that place? A store for porn?"

 [Madarame] "Well, to put it in your terms, yes."

 [Kasukabe] "Are those stores over there the same thing?"

 [Kousaka] "That's right."

 [Kasukabe] "This place is full of porn shops. So all these people around us are going to go home and #*&!(%... Wow, Akihabara is such a dirty town."

 [Madarame] "Hey, how dare you! This is a paradise that gives us hopes and dreams. It's heaven on earth."

[Kasukabe] "Dreams? What you buy are porno games and porno books. You're just here to satisfy your horniness."

[Madarame] "No, that's not true. The universe is about love. What we're seeking is the fantasy of love. We're trying to achieve something that we can't achieve with real women."

[Kasukabe] "I see. But what do you actually do at home with your porn?"

 [Madarame] "Umm..."

 [Kasukabe] "Come on, answer me."

I was going to ask Ogiue-san, but she was nowhere to be seen. I started looking around, and found her gazing at a fanzine shop.

 [Sasahara] "Did you want to go in?"

 [Ogiue] "...N-no."

I couldn't help but laugh. Ogiue-san glared up at me.

 [Sasahara] "I'm sorry. Let's go in. I want to look, too."

So we went into the fanzine shop. Meanwhile...

It really was Madarame-san. I found out later that he had followed us.

 [Madarame] "That was close."

 [Kousaka] "Maybe we got a little too close."

And it wasn't just Madarame-san. Kousaka-kun, Kasukabe-san, and Kuchiki-kun were with him, too. Sheesh, they really like spying on people.

 [Kasukabe] "Why are so many guys giving Sasa-yan such an evil look?"

 [Madarame] "The people of this town aren't exactly welcoming to couples."

 [Kasukabe] "Whoa, shallow!"

They were wondering what to do, since we had gone into the fanzine store.

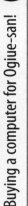

Buying a computer for Ogiue-san!

 [Kuchiki] "Captain. I accidentally found this."

Kuchiki-kun handed a fanzine to Madarame-san. It was the fanzine we'd sold at Comic-Fest last summer. We didn't have stores carry them, so that meant someone had sold it.

 [Madarame] "I'm so glad Kugayama didn't come."

Apparently, the fanzine was being resold for only 100 yen (cry).

 [Madarame] "Anyway, just hide it. I don't want them to see it. The shock would be too much for them."

 [Kuchiki] "Hide it? Where?"

 [Madarame] "Just hold on to it."

When we were walking away from the women's section, it happened.

I heard a familiar voice and turned around in time to see Kuchiki-kun.

 [Sasahara] "Oh, Kuchiki-kun. I didn't know you were coming here today."

 [Kuchiki] "Oh...uh, um..."

Kuchiki-kun looked distinctly worried. Nervously, he glanced toward the bookshelves in the back.

 [Madarame] "Idiot, don't look over here."

I could barely make out Madarame-san's Akihabara outfit, but it

 [Kousaka] "Saki-chan, those are two separate issues."

 [Kasukabe] (Smiling like she's about to cry)

The upshot was that Madarame-san and gang decided to follow us into the fanzine shop.

 [Kasukabe] "Hey, wait."

Kasukabe-san was left alone on the street. She tried to go inside, but her feet refused to move.

See, the picture of the girls in front of the store was blocking her way.

There were girls who were smiling right at her. There were girls showing her their breasts. There were girls seducing her...

 [Kasukabe] "There's no way!"

 [Madarame] "Oh, there they are."

Madarame-san and gang found us in the women's section. They hid in the men's section, spying on us from behind some bookshelves.

 [Madarame] "Sasahara is acting scared. And he looks kind of shaky. I'm worried he's going to faint."

I wish he would leave me alone. (Well, that was what I thought when he told me later.) But I was supposed to be accompanying Ogiue-san, so I couldn't just leave her and go to the men's section alone. I could only stand next to her, red-faced, while she carefully looked through the zines.

[Madarame] "Now, Sasahara, that's not true. I just came to make sure you were able to get all the parts I wrote down."

 [Sasahara] "Then why didn't you come with her in the first place?"

 [Madarame] "Look, you can't keep leaving stuff up to me. You're the Genshiken president. Your presidential duties include instructing the newbies."

 [Sasahara] "But that's..."

 [Madarame] "You can't keep relying on me."

 [Sasahara] "..."

It was annoying that they got off the hook so easily, but there was no point in trying to get an apology.

(I'm sure Madarame-san's heart was racing as he talked to me, though.)

 [Madarame] (Phew. I got out of that one smoothly. Thank God.)

That's what the look on his face said to me.

 [Madarame] "Anyway, I started thinking that maybe I should help out after all. So I'll take over from here."

 [Sasahara] "Thank you. But how does that explain why Kasukabe-san is here?"

was enough to tell me that it was the same one I thought I'd seen earlier.

I yelled at the guy wearing the Akihabara outfit, who was making a hasty retreat out the door. Ogiue-san hadn't caught what was going on, but she came with me.

 [Sasahara] "Madarame-san? What are you doing?"

Once outside, Madarame-san finally gave up and spoke to me.

 [Madarame] "Well, I just felt like shopping, that's all."

 [Sasahara] "And why are Kousaka-kun and Kasukabe-san here, too?"

 [Kasukabe] "We're just on a date."

 [Kousaka] "Yeah, a date."

 [Sasahara] "A *date*? Kasukabe-san, you said that you'd never come to Akihabara."

 [Kasukabe] "Well, you know, I just felt like it..."

[Sasahara] "...you guys followed us, didn't you?"

[Madarame] "You make it sound like we're committing a crime."

[Sasahara] "You guys were having fun watching me take Ogiue-san all around Akihabara, weren't you?"

 [Ogiue] "!"

nicely, and the store honors warranties. And it's the cheapest to buy it here."

The clerks echoed what Madarame said—yes, the parts are fine. I still thought it was fishy.

I took a look at the notes Madarame-san had written, and they really did say to come to this store.

And when I think about going to that store, just Ogiue-san and me... I guess it might be true that Madarame-san decided to help us, in the end.

 [Madarame] "Well, I'll go over there and get the parts."

 [Kasukabe] "Please hurry. If I stay here too long, I'm going to age faster... I'm going to wilt..."

Madarame-san went to the back counter to explain something. (There was a lot of gesturing going on.) Ogiue-san stood next to me, looking at Madarame-san.

 [Ogiue] "..."

 [Sasahara] "You know, Ogiue-san..."

 [Ogiue] "Oh! Y-yes?"

[Sasahara] "I should've asked sooner, but are you sure you're okay with this?"

[Ogiue] "With what?"

[Sasahara] "Buying a computer. Because what you

 [Madarame] "Urk..."

 [Kasukabe] "I have my reasons. I thought it looked interesting, so I followed you guys, that's all."

 [Madarame] (How evil.)

The store Madarame-san took us to was a hole in the wall, hidden among some old buildings. You had to take an elevator to reach the store itself, but it was too small to hold all of us. Even when we split up into two groups, it was still too small. It didn't help that it made scary creaking noises as we went up.

When the elevator doors opened, we found ourselves in the store. The clerks welcomed us in broken Japanese.

 [Kasukabe] "Whoa, they're not native. And the store is really small and dark. Seems fishy to me."

[Sasahara] "Ha ha..."

[Kasukabe] "Is the computer going to work with parts you buy from here?"

It's okay, it'll work, said the employees, with a heavy accent.

[Kousaka] "Saki-chan, they could hear you."

[Madarame] "The store might look fishy, but the parts are fine. They customize

[Madarame] "Hey, Ogiue-san. Can you come over here? I have some questions."

 [Ogiue] "Um, okay."

Ogiue-san ran to the counter to talk to Madarame-san. I could hear her answering his questions in a small but assertive voice, so I was relieved.

 [Kasukabe] "What, did you fall in love with her?"

 [Sasahara] "What are you saying? Of course not."

 [Kasukabe] "Why not? You guys did go on a date."

 [Sasahara] "It's not a date."

 [Kasukabe] "Sheesh. How boring."

Sigh.

Ogiue-san was able to get her computer for a very reasonable price, thanks to Madarame-san's favorite store, so she bought the software for Photoshop and the "Otaru" DVD.

And then, about a week after she got her computer...

 [Kasukabe] "Ogiue, how's your computer? Are you using it?"

[Ogiue] "Yes, I am."

[Kasukabe] "Are you playing porn games?"

originally wanted was a DVD player."

 [Ogiue] "Yes. But..."

 [Sasahara] "But now it's become a computer, and there's all these specifications that Sempai thinks you should have."

 [Ogiue] "Yeah..."

 [Sasahara] "Look, even if someone's your sempai, you have to say no to things you don't want. You're the one buying it."

 [Ogiue] "..."

 [Sasahara] "We should call it off. I don't think it's a good idea to buy it if you're not sure you want it."

 [Ogiue] "No, hang on."

 [Sasahara] "!"

[Ogiue] "It's okay. I want it. I did want to work with Photoshop, and if I can watch DVDs on it, then it's fine."

[Sasahara] "Really? If you're sure you're okay with it, then that's good."

[Ogiue] "Yes. Um, thank you."

[Sasahara] "Hmm?"

Buying a computer for Ogiue-san!

[Ogiue] "Of course not!"

[Kasukabe] "...well, I guess you wouldn't."

[Sasahara] (Wry smile)

[Kasukabe] "Then what are you using it for?"

[Ogiue] "To watch DVDs and to draw."

[Kasukabe] "So, exactly what you bought it for. What do you draw?"

[Ogiue] "I got nostalgic when I watched the DVD, so I'm drawing Otaru and Sakeou..."

[Sasahara] "Huh?"

[Kasukabe] "Hmm—I guess you're not so different."

[Ogiue] "Huh? Huh? Huh?"

[Ohno] "Heh...almighty otaku girl."

[Ogiue] "!"

Tosanbou/Community Center Sunday Market

Tosanbou is short for Tokyo Toritsu Sangyo Boeki Center (Tokyo Metropolitan Industrial Trade Center). The one they're talking about is located off the JR Yamanote Line at Hamamatsu-cho Station, and has a hall that's frequently used for midsized fanzine events.

____-Only Event

Comiket is a fanzine event that covers all genres, but there are other fanzine events that focus on certain subjects or characters. At those events the participants all have common interests, so people usually get along even though they're meeting each other for the first time.

Mid-Island

The island refers to a block of booths for circles to use. It usually consists of a table and two chairs. Booths that are more in the center of the hall are called "mid-island." The booths at the edge of an island are called "corner of an island."

Porn Parody

Porn parodies usually take a manga or anime aimed at a male audience and put the characters in pornographic situations you wouldn't find in the original series.

Sketchbook (Sukebu)

Sukebu is short for sketch-book, but it also refers to illustrations drawn by the fan-zine artist for the person who buys the fanzine. Since there are time constraints and page number constraints, it's against the rules to give a sketchbook with a one-sided layout.

Photoshop

Photoshop is a piece of software developed by Adobe Systems. You can check the quality of the picture using the high image quality on the screen, and work from that. It's a must-have for fanzine creators and professional designers alike.

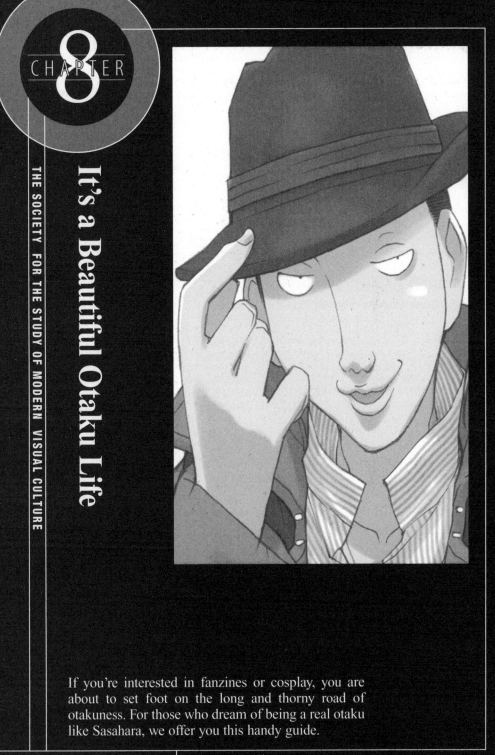

CHAPTER 8

It's a Beautiful Otaku Life

THE SOCIETY FOR THE STUDY OF MODERN VISUAL CULTURE

If you're interested in fanzines or cosplay, you are about to set foot on the long and thorny road of otakuness. For those who dream of being a real otaku like Sasahara, we offer you this handy guide.

GENSHIKEN OFFICIAL BOOK

WHAT'S THAT?

SO, WE'LL SAVE SASAHARA'S "BIG EVENT" FOR LATER, EH?

WHY DON'T WE GO DOWN THE MAIN DRAG FIRST? AND CHECK STUFF OUT ALONG THE WAY.

Akihabara is the holy land for otaku in Japan and around the world. As "Genshiken" reminded us time and again, Akiba is overflowing with otaku entertainment of every kind.

Shinjuku, Ikebukuro, and Akihabara are the three most wondrous districts in Tokyo. Of the three, Akihabara is best known as the electronics district, but it's also an ideal source for comics and doujinshi, and the hobby and game shops that fuel otaku life. During the weekend, the Akihabara JR Station swarms with pilgrims from all over Japan.

Our heroes' first stop is the main drag, Chuou-douri (Central Street). This street is lined with major stores like Sofmap and LAOX. Crowds of people converge on the storefronts to watch popular video game demos; just by walking down the street, you can get a sense of what's popular in Akiba. For beginners, understanding Chuou-dori is an essential first step. Mineshima-san, who handles PR for Tora no Ana, says, "Our store and Messe Sanoh face Chuou-dori, and they create an open atmosphere that is accessible to everyone. It's the best environment for beginners to buy their first doujinshi."

Meanwhile, if you venture onto the side streets that branch out from Chuou-dori, there are cosplay shops and other stores that delve deeper into the otaku world.

A Healthy Otaku Life Begins with a Pilgrimage to Akihabara

HEY, SASAHARA. YOU'RE ALL BY YOURSELF? THAT'S RARE.

ON A SECRET SHOPPING EXPEDITION?

NO...

It takes a bit of courage for Akiba novices to explore by themselves, but there are plenty of Akiba-related guidebooks these days, so you can do your research and decide which stores you want to check out first. Most of the stores have extensive websites, so those can also be useful reference tools.

When you get tired from walking around, take a break at a trendy cosplay café. These are becoming more popular because you can sit and look at cute girls in cosplay for the low cost of a cup of coffee. But if you drop by when an otaku event is going on, brace yourself for a long line to get into the café. Also, if you're waiting for a midnight sale, manga cafés are your friend. They'll probably be crowded, but you can kill some time there without spending a lot.

Your initial excursions to Akiba may lack focus, but as you go more often you'll begin to have regular stores that meet your needs. Then Akiba will truly welcome you with open arms!

"Comic Tora no Ana Store 1" TEL 03-5294-0123
4-3-1 Soto-Kanda, Chiyoda-ku, Tokyo
Store hours: 11:00 – 21:00 (10:00 - 21:00 on
Fri, Sat, Sun, and holidays), open year round.

A Place to Check Out When You Go to Akiba!

Otaku Palace
Tora no Ana

Tora no Ana is a popular store with three locations in Akihabara. The flagship store is Store 1, which sells merchandise like trading cards and figures, as well as mature comics, magazines, and doujinshi—a wide selection of must-have items for the otaku life! Store 2 sells used books, and Store 3 sells doujinshi and mature books. Collectively, they fill the needs of everyone from novices to hard-core fans.

really helped their popularity explode," says Mineshima-san. Putting them down on paper is a way to make the images and stories you'd imagined for your favorite moe characters real. It's not surprising that this idea captured the hearts of otaku everywhere, and these days there are recognizable genres and divisions.

Right now the two big genres are the cute, bishoujo-centered type of story, and the more realistic, more "hard-core" kind. Mineshima-san notes that "there is a lack of killer titles right now. Titles like 'Sister Princess' and 'Martian Successor Nadesico' were hits, but there hasn't been anything with a huge influence. Recently, girly games have been bigger hits than anime. This will probably continue to be the situation for some time." In the end, the struggle for dominance results in many titles and art styles being shoved aside, but this competition creates a good situation for readers.

The otaku heart is captured by both moe-related and hard-core S&M stories

Lately, "Genshiken" has been very focused on the club's creation of a doujinshi for Comic-Fest. The fanzines they talk about are self-published books that like-minded fans create to sell at events like Comiket. This is a vital aspect of the otaku path which simply cannot be ignored. "Current doujinshi are mostly based on preexisting anime and manga, as well as video game characters. Hits like 'Sailor Moon' and 'Evangelion'

Madarame's
Doujinshi-Buying Guide

◀ Fanzines can be selected by either series or author. As you become familiar with the market, you'll discover your own favorite authors.

HE DOESN'T LOOK AT THE PRICE.

FLIP FLIP FLIP!!

UH...

JUST LOOK AT THE SPEED WITH WHICH HE SCANS THE LATEST ISSUE OF E.E. SAKURA.

Some buying and selling goes on online, but buying fanzines at events like Comiket or at fanzine shops is more typical. Events should be the first line of attack, since they offer a wide variety of titles that can't be purchased at the stores.

▼ Discovering a fanzine is a once-in-a-lifetime opportunity. If you like what you see, you should try to purchase as many copies as you can so you don't regret missing out later. This is the position taken by true otaku!

▲ Fanzine shops have sample books that preview some of the interior art. If the cover catches your eye, make sure to take a look at what's inside.

HE BUYS EVERY "SISTER ANGEL" ZINE THAT HE CAN GET HIS HANDS ON.

HE CHOOSES SOLELY BASED ON THE ORIGINAL SERIES.

HE LIKES "SISTER ANGEL."

I COULD BUY ONE OR TWO OF THE 2000 YEN BOOKS, OR FOUR OR FIVE OF THE ONES THAT ONLY COST A FEW HUNDRED YEN.

SHOULD I CHOOSE BASED ON THE ART, OR THE SERIES THE ZINE IS BASED ON...

I'VE GOTTA WEIGH MY OPTIONS...

▲ Price varies according to paper quality, printing, and page count, but ultimately it's the author's call. They can cost anywhere from 600 yen to several thousand yen.

Sasahara's Guide to Making a Fanzine

◀ Booth layout for the event. Groups that may have long lines are placed along the walls, and those that won't are placed in an island in the middle.

▲ In order to participate in an event like Comiket, you need to fill out an application form in advance. For popular events, you also need to make it through a screening process.

▼ You receive notice that you've been accepted as a participant. The acceptance package includes information about the dates and your booth location. Your adventure begins here!

hundred? Fewer?) and whether you want to go with photocopying or offset printing. With printers, it's normal to pay up front. You reserve a time and try to choose a deadline, but if you're participating in a big event like Comiket you may have to be flexible about the deadline, since the printers will be dealing with a lot of orders. When you place your order, the price will vary depending on whether the pages are all in full color, or only the covers, or if the

It's possible to make a fanzine on your own, but we'll focus on how a group creates one. First, you figure out what its content will be. The basic rule is that everyone involved should like the same series, and preferably also be fans of the same characters. Then you need to decide what your take on the original series is going to be (a parody? An erotic manga?), and begin thinking about structure. You need to establish how many copies will be printed (several

7/27	DEADLINE
28	5% PRICE INCREASE
29	
30	
31	10% PRICE INCREASE
8/1	
2	
3	15% PRICE INCREASE
4	
5	20% PRICE INCREASE
6	FURTHER PRICE INCREASE NEGOTIABLE

▲ You create a schedule when you make an appointment with the printer. Some printers won't charge extra if you submit your materials late.

▲ Taking the completed manuscript to the printers. Here they check through your materials, and if there are no problems you can just wait for the final printed product. You can also submit your fanzine to them digitally.

▶ Having the printed books delivered directly to the event hall is called "direct delivery." This is a standard procedure.

▲ Determine the structure of the fanzine early on. It's an important step if you plan on making a profit at an event.

▲ Whether or not you can break even and cover the cost of printing depends on how the fanzine sells. Some people cosplay to attract customers.

the fanzine will be ready on the delivery date. If the print run is small, it might be safest to pick up your package at the printer, even though it may be extra work. But if you plan to sell it at an event like Comiket, then the procedure is to have it sent directly to the event hall. No matter what kind of zine you chose to create, holding the finished product that you've worked on together is sure to give you a sense of accomplishment.

whole book is in black and white. If you're making the fanzine to sell at an event, the printing method and price affect how well it sells, so choose wisely! Once you've made your printing arrangements, you turn your attention to completing the artwork by the deadline.

When you have a completed manuscript ready to print, number all of the pages to prevent them from being lost or printed out of order. If there are no problems,

Ogiue: "I Hate Yaoi!"

▲ Not all characters that appear in yaoi doujinshi are good-looking men. There are genres that cater to all tastes, whether you prefer bald guys or older men...

▲ Don't take them lightly because they're for women. Some are more graphic than the mature fanzines for men.

◄ Even though yaoi is becoming more socially acceptable, it's still hard to come out as a yaoi fan.

than zines aimed at male audiences.

The girls later saw potential in various Shonen Jump titles like "Dragon Ball Z" and "Slam Dunk." In recent years, the word "yaoi" has become mainstream, and the genre can't be dismissed.

Perhaps this is a good time to mention that male otaku and female yaoi-loving otaku (known as *fujoshi*, which literally means "rotten girl") are as incompatible as oil and water.

"Yaoi" (stories depicting homosexual content, usually between two good-looking men) is a common unifier among otaku girls. Its frequent explicitness would seem likely to keep it underground, but in fact yaoi fanzines were what sustained the fanzine movement in the '80s. At the time, "Captain Tsubasa" and "Six God Combination Godmars" were popular source material for yaoi fanzines, which were more common

Comics

The Product at the Root of Other Multimedia

Right from the beginning, comics have been the basic expression of otaku culture. In the late 1980s the "anime manga" (anime images used to create a comic version of a series) format was established, and it still continues to be used. More recently, video games and OVAs have been added to the mix, but comics are still the heart of multimedia properties. Of the different manga genres, like shonen and seinen, it's the shonen magazines that are most popular. The big three weekly shonen magazines ("Shonen Magazine," "Shonen Jump," and "Shonen Sunday") regularly produce popular series. "Magazine" is especially popular among male readers because of its many beautiful girl characters, while "Jump" strategically uses good-looking male characters to draw in female audiences. (That is the driving force behind the aforementioned yaoi explosion.) On the other hand, monthly shonen magazines cater to more serious otaku readers, with their higher proportion of moe girls.

"Street Fighter II" was the first of the modern fight games

The fight game era can trace its origin to the Famicom age in the mid-'80s. In those days, most games were simple side-scrolling, beat-the-bad-guy titles like "Kung-Fu Master." The game that popularized the idea of letting players fight each other was "Ultimate Muscle Tag Match," in which super-deformed superheroes duke it out in a square ring, moving up and down as well as left and right. Its simple controls and special moves helped many people get hooked on the game. But the main arena of fight games was the arcade. While other popular kinds of games were being ported to Famicom and Super Famicom, fight games fell behind due to

LET ME MAKE THIS PERFECTLY CLEAR. IT'S NOT JUST THAT YOU CAN DO THINGS IN GAMES THAT "AREN'T POSSIBLE IN REAL LIFE."

A VIDEO GAME CONSISTS OF NOTHING BUT NUMBERS AND CODE, AND COMBINING THAT WITH HUMAN IMAGINATION IN ORDER TO CREATE SEXUAL DESIRE REQUIRES A FAR MORE ADVANCED INTELLECTUAL CAPACITY THAN SIMPLE HUMAN PHYSICAL ATTRACTION.

their higher system requirements. The fight game that broke through and became popular on the Super Famicom was "Street Fighter II," which featured full-height, beautiful characters fighting in 2-D. Attractive female characters also helped bring in more fans. And the concept of creating special

SORRY, I'LL GO HOME IN A MINUTE.

WOULD YOU PLEASE?

CHAPTER 17
LIFE OR DEATH

GAMES (Fight Games)

The joy of controlling the girls in the game

Games (Fight Games)

moves and attack combos by using button combinations gave players an increased capacity for improving their gameplay by practicing. This overall package became the standard for later fight games.

In the mid-'90s, 3-D polygon fight games on the next-generation consoles became the norm. Games like "Tekken" and "Virtua Fighter" used realistic characters that were capable of more complex moves that required a higher level of skill with the controls. This high threshold gradually made fight games the domain of hard-core users. The number of pretty girl characters increased, with many of them fighting in sexy outfits; at around the same time, cosplaying as characters like Chun-Li from "Street Fighter II" took off. The current wave of fight games includes some of the classics, battle games based on "Mobile Suit Gundam," and survival games like "Biohazard (Resident Evil)." All of them are popular among otaku because your skill levels depend on how much you play.

Serious players like complicated controls that challenge dexterity

These days, approximately 20 new girly or porn game titles hit the shelves each month. It's difficult to pinpoint exactly when it started, but the trend definitely came from the PC games that were made for the PC88 and MSX computers that were popular in the '80s. One of the games that helped the fledgling movement along was a game called "Rance" (released by Alice Soft) that came on the heels of hits like "Dragon Quest." The game featured plenty of pretty girl characters, and its goal was to save a land occupied only by women from an evil threat. At around the same time, porno and girly games started to be released for the PC, one after another. Among them was a revolutionary game called "Classmate," released by Elf in 1992. It was a successful teenage romance game and sold over 200,000 copies. But it wasn't only the erotic elements that determined success: an emphasis on story and gameplay were also incorporated into console video games, and led to the mega-hit "Tokimeki Memorial," released for the Super Famicom in 1994. Among the home entertainment systems, one that put a lot of energy into

Girly games became popular after "Classmate" was a hit

GAMES

(Porn Games/ Girly Games)

The enjoyment of a simulated romance that takes place in your imagination

girly games was the Sega Saturn.

They released games like "Sakura Wars" and "Sentimental Graffiti" that were original to their system, rather than being ported in from PC games. When the PlayStation 2 era began, this trend became even stronger. Erotic games are often centered on moe (or "little sister") characters. These days, PC games are often developed with the intention of porting them to home entertainment systems.

Currently, "little sister" characters from games like "Sister Princess" are in vogue, but other popular games fall under the "humiliation game" genre, which focuses only on the erotic aspects. These games involve no romance, aiming to humiliate and dominate attractive girls. A

Hooray for porno game characters! A new era dawns

leading series called "Shuusaku" was so successful that it was turned into an anime. But otaku tend to prefer girly games with moe characters over the visually realistic humiliation games.

There are plenty of fanzines that draw on well-loved characters from porn games, and tie-in figurines and merchandise are common.

Some video game characters have a more impressive following than their anime counterparts. These days, porn games are considered an important part of otaku culture in their own right.

Anime may be the most recognized symbol of the otaku. Its golden age was in the '80s, when there were fewer media options. Anime filled TV's prime-time slots, and every year there were new animated films of incredible quality and influence. At the same time, the word "otaku" gained real recognition.

Otaku culture itself focused on two key genres during this period: realistic robot series, led by Sunrise's "Mobile Suit Gundam," and magical girl series like "Minky Momo." Factor in the influence of the "Shonen Jump" lineup, and you can see the power of the anime boom. The wave lost momentum in the '90s, however, as anime shows were pushed

Waiting for the next "Evangelion"

into late-afternoon and late-night slots and had to rely on direct-to-video releases. But that falling-out with the mainstream generated more titles that were created specifically to appeal to the hard-core fans; in a way, it was a dream come true for the otaku. Anime regained some of its power with "Neon Genesis Evangelion," which featured a complicated storyline and subplots, as well as characters who appealed to the general public instead of otaku alone. The series' effect on otaku culture is still being felt, with related

Anime / Otaku Merchandise

books still being released every year. Unfortunately, nothing with similar impact and staying power has been created since.

Limited editions and first print runs are popular

As seen in "Genshiken," one way otaku show their desire to be with their favorite characters all the time is to have huge wallscrolls, calendars, or posters covering their walls. A favorite place to display these pieces of art is on the ceiling right above the bed. Trading cards and phone cards are also favorite collectibles, with trading cards soaring in popularity in recent years. Rare items are no longer in as much demand as they once were, but they still go for high prices in online auctions.

Other sought-after merchandise includes limited-edition items that come with the initial releases of games and DVDs and which can't be bought separately in stores. People who line up to buy new things on their release date are often after those limited-edition, first-print-run items. It's common for one person to buy up several copies.

At anime stores, mainstay merchandise like animation cels and original drawings are still popular,

but these days more fans are in search of swag relating to video games than anime. This is just another indication that girly games are a huge part of the modern otaku trends.

OTAKU MERCHANDISE

The otaku mind-set includes wanting to have reminders of a favorite character

In the beginning, people dressed up as characters to stand out at fanzine events, but cosplay became its own separate activity as it caught on. In the '90s it became a widely accepted hobby, as evidenced by the emergence of cosplay parties.

There's some debate about exactly when it all started, but "Urusei Yatsura" cosplay was what brought it into the public eye. Before then, there had been people who wore Gundam crew uniforms or tried to imitate

COSPLAY
Fulfilling the desire to be like the character you love

Did it all start with Lum?

Arare-chan's look, but it was Lum's sexy costume that had the most impact. Since then, cosplay of anime, manga, and video game characters has been a staple of fanzine events. On the Internet, meanwhile, cosplayers create websites to showcase their photos.

There are certain cosplay outfits that

Cosplay News

Helmet
The Rikkyuoin High School emblem is prominently displayed. The sides of the helmet have ventilation holes to increase airflow. The construction is detailed, but the helmet is lighter than it looks, and is cushioned inside to fit snugly on your head.

Armband
The armband stretches to accommodate arms of any size. The blouse doesn't sag, and the starched look emphasizes the president's strict appearance.

Ribbon
The ribbon is already shaped into a bow, so it doesn't need to be retied for each wearing. You simply attach it to the buttons on the bottom of the collar, so it doesn't take much time to get ready.

Emblem on Chest
The Rikkyuoin High emblem is machine-embroidered to maximize detail.

Skirt
In order to maximize volume, the president's skirt has 14 pleats instead of a normal skirt's six. You can wear a pannier (sold separately) underneath to complete the look.

Toys made for adults, appealing to the otaku's desire to collect

Usually the term "figures" refers to dolls made of PVC and soft vinyl plastic. But in the otaku world, the ideal figures are the garage-kit versions of characters from girly games and anime. Historically, the hard-core garage-kit fans were seen as a unique subgroup, but after the massive success of "Neon Genesis Evangelion" that group became inextricably linked to anime otaku. These days garage kits are made for any title with beautiful girl characters (like Rei Ayanami from "Evangelion"), dressing

Garage kits: the ultimate figures

them in school uniforms, swimsuits, and various other outfits. The best part of garage kits is the creator's new designs for the characters, but it's most common for the figures to be designed erotically. The more skin a figure shows, the higher the price. If you're like Tanaka and have the skill to complete one, you might want to challenge yourself with a kit instead of buying a pre-made figure.

Other than the pretty girl characters, figures based

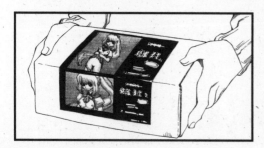

on "Gundam" and other robot titles from large manufacturers are popular.

The current trend with robot action figures is to

THE WAY THE FIGURE SEEMS A BIT AWKWARD AND UNBALANCED REALLY HELPS ACCENTUATE THAT "KID SISTER" LOOK.

HAVING HER DRESS UP IN THESE CLOTHES SHE BORROWED FROM THE MAIN CHARACTER'S LITTLE SISTER... ACTUALLY CHANGES HER INTO A KIND OF "KID SISTER" CHARACTER.

THE SIZE OF THE OUTFIT IS PERFECT FOR SHOWING OFF THE SOFT CURVACEOUS SHAPE OF HER BODY.

CLICK

Products designed to make you want them

have the arms and legs move, or to have additional gimmicks included. There are limited-release figures, as well as bonus figures included with the initial releases of some video games. These are all designed to appeal to the otaku desire to build a collection. Some figures can be bought online, but for the full experience you should also visit a specialty store in Akihabara.

On the other end of the spectrum from garage kits are toys that cost only a few hundred yen. Toys like this are often packaged with snacks, but they can still be high quality when companies like Kaiyodo are involved in making them. They can be anything from animals or bugs to anime characters.

Most of these toys are available only for a limited time, and you don't know which one you'll get when you make your purchase, so it takes a lot of time and money to complete a series. Figure specialty stores also sell this kind of toy, so you can fill in the gaps in your collection there. The rarer figures are sometimes sold in online auctions. Unlike garage kits, these toys are all about the joy of collecting.

YOU HAVE TO BUILD THESE YOURSELF.

PLASTIC MODELS AND TOYS ARE TOTALLY DIFFERENT.

OH, SO THEY'RE NOT AS GOOD AS TOYS.

Gundam plastic models (aka "Gunpla") were sold in the '80s after the series aired on TV. The unprecedented realism of the mobile suit models, combined with their low price of 300 yen, made them sell out all over Japan. Their trendiness played a part in those sales, but it was their high quality that ultimately beat the competition.

Gunpla, which are usually made in 1:144 scale, went through a new boom every time the show was rebroadcast. After all of the mobile suits that appeared in the series had been made, test models like Zaku Canon and Acguy were also released.

The quality of Gundam plastic models was infinitely superior

UM... DID I ASK FOR AN EXPLANA-TION?

IN SUMMER AND WINTER, IT'S REALLY HARD TO CONTROL TEMPERATURE AND HUMIDITY LEVELS.

A HA HA HA HA.

I TOLD YOU, I DIDN'T ASK!

...IS THAT IT CAN SUD-DENLY GET SO COLD THAT IT'S HARD TO GO ON PAINTING.

AND THE REA-SON THAT FALL IS NO GOOD...

YOU EVEN MADE A PRINTOUT...

TAKE IT UP TO THE NEXT LEVEL
(EASY STEPS TO SUCCESS)

THIS IS THE BEST TIME OF YEAR FOR MAKING PLASTIC MODELS.

Gundam Plastic Models

> AH! YEAH... SURE DID.

> DID YOU MAKE THIS ONE, TANAKA?

> HMM...

> YOINK

"Z Gundam" and "Gundam ZZ" aired in 1985 and 1986, but by then the fad was dying down. And then, in 1995, the Master Grade

The ultimate Gunpla: the PG!

Series was created to celebrate the series' 15-year anniversary.

With the MG series, the models' standard scale was changed from 1:144 to 1:100. This made it possible to include new details and ranges of movement, and the MG were a big hit among the 20- and 30-somethings who had been in elementary school during the first Gunpla boom.

In 1999, to celebrate "Gundam"'s 20th anniversary, the 1:60 scale Perfect Grade Series was released. It re-created the internal mechanics of the mobile suits, and featured a sensor camera that lit up; this sort of irresistible addition made it the ultimate Gunpla experience. Currently one PG model is released each year, along with one 1:100 scale MG model and one 1:144 scale HGUC (High Grade Universal Century) model. These three new annual models carry Gunpla's popularity forward each year. The joy of building and having a realistic mobile suit continues to appeal to the hearts of otaku.

> THUMP THUMP THUMP THUMP

AKIHABARA"

This story takes place one Friday soon after Kanji purchased a PC so he could play porn games. Written by KASIN

Friday, in a certain month on a certain day at 1:00 P.M. in Akihabara.

Madarame: Ahh, there's nothing like the smell of a Friday (*1) in Akiba (*2).

Kanji: There's a lot of people around for a Friday.

Madarame: Well, yeah. It's Friday *and* the end of the month (*3).

Kanji: Huh? Is that important?

Madarame: Payday's usually on the 25th, right? That makes this the first Friday after payday, so it's the biggest day for new porno games (*4). Of course Akiba's gonna be bubbling over!

Kanji: All of these people are here to buy porno games? Seriously?

Madarame: Seventy percent of the people in Akiba on a Friday morning (*5) are here for their porno game fix. That's basic math! That 30-year-old who looks like he's in showbiz was carrying a paper bag with a poster (*6) sticking out, right? And that college student's messenger bag is full of it. And *that* guy in the suit is probably playing hooky from his sales job to turn this morning's direct-deposit pay into porn. Yep, the video game makers know today's the best day to put things out.

Kanji: So that's why there are 27 new releases today (*7).

▶ "Akiba-type Girlfriend" (Tech Arts G J ? Brand) A romantic comedy adventure about an otaku's awkward attempts to turn the non-otaku girl he likes into someone more suited to him—i.e., another otaku.

2: Akiba
A nickname for Akihabara. The name originates from a deity brought from "Akihadaigongen" in Shizuoka during the Meiji Era. It was originally pronounced "Akibahara" or "Akibappara," which is why "Akiba" came to be the short form. The name now refers to the immediate area around the JR Akihabara Station, the Chuou-dori from Mansei Bridge to Tokyo Metro Ginza Line Suehiro-cho Station, and the "Akihabara Electric District" on both sides of Chuou-dori. It was originally a household appliances district, became an electronics district, and is still in touch with those roots in its current incarnation as a thriving hobby district. Many porno games are set in Akiba; one of them, "Akiba-type Girlfriend" (Tech Arts), is similar to the "Genshiken" world. It's highly recommended to readers interested in porn games.

1: Friday
Porn games (PC games for customers 18 and older) are released on Fridays due to distribution issues. For the same reason, console games are released on Thursdays. Akihabara shops have an agreement not to presell erotic games before the release date.

Hunting the Best Porn Games in "TGIF: Moe in Akihabara"

Hunting the Best Porn Games in

"TGIF: MOE IN

Madarame: Nice, Sasahara—you've done your research. How much money do you have?

Kanji: My parents sent me my allowance yesterday, but I only brought 15,000 yen with me.

Madarame: So that's two games at Akiba prices (*8).

Kanji: Yeah. "Puriimo Seven" (*9) is my default (*10) choice, but for my other one... (Taking out a shopping list) ...I'm going to choose between these three after I take a look at them.

Madarame: Hmm... "Class Maid Fallen Angel of the Classroom," "Beautiful Sisters on the Groping Express Train," "Night Courting Academy ~ Girls' Dormitory of Perversion." (*11) I see! (grin)

Kanji: H-hey!

Madarame: Hey, that's normal. Gotta have one game that's for jacking off (*12). (Drawing on the week's release schedule sheet with a ballpoint pen) Then I'll go with one of these five. "Puriimo" comes with a first print exclusive (*13) key art illustration book, so I'll keep that on my list. But otherwise, we should make sure we don't get the same things. Kugayama and Kousaka already told me what they're getting, so we should be able to cover all of the good titles. Make sure you lend us the one you buy, all right?

7: 27 new releases
That was the actual number of releases on the last Friday of a certain month. It's not unusual to see 30 titles released in a month.

6: Poster
A poster that is included on a first-come, first-served basis when purchasing new software. Most titles available at specialty stores come with one, so it's not uncommon to see otaku with five or six posters sticking out of their bags and backpacks.

5: Morning
Akiba's specialty stores open at 11:00 A.M. But when big titles are slated for release they may open at midnight or in the early morning.

4: Porno games
Refers to adult PC games that cannot be sold to minors. The term "porno games" is the most straightforward, while video game magazines refer to them as "girly games." But some people prefer not to use either term for games that are less than 10% erotic, such as romance games or the increasingly popular adultery games. Other terms used are "adult games," "over-18 games," and "gal games." Of those, "gal games" refers to pretty girl games that can be played by people of all ages.

3: Friday at the end of the month
Some companies have their payday on the 20th, but it's more common to have it on the 25th. So the first Friday after payday, which is the last Friday of the month, is the monthly purchase date for porn games. It can usually just be referred as the last Friday of each month, but if the 25th falls on a Saturday or Sunday, payday falls on the 23rd and there are two Fridays after payday. In that case, the titles being released that month are split between the two weeks.

Kanji: That's fine… (Peeking at Madarame's list) Isn't that fourth one supposed to be a bit of a land mine (*14)?

Madarame: Hmph! Even if they think there's a land mine ahead, real men keep going.

At a shop on Chuou-dori, close to Suehiro-cho Station

Madarame: I can't find "Puriimo" anywhere.

Kanji: Maybe it was delayed (*15)?

Madarame: No way. I checked the info sites (*16) last night before I went to sleep, and it didn't mention anything about that… It couldn't have sold out before noon, could it?

??: No, it was recalled (*17).

Kanji: Kousaka?

Madarame: Kousaka!

And there's Kousaka, holding a large paper bag with several posters sticking out.

Kousaka: There was an error with the mosaic (*18), so the stores all had to recall it by noon. I pre-ordered my copy (*19), so I came down to get it before then.

Madarame: Geez, for real?

▶ **"Mizuiro" (Neko Neko Soft)**

Neko Neko Soft, Circus (maker of "Da Capo"), and Witch (maker of "Milkyway") are three companies based in Saitama. They are referred to as the Saitama Coalition.

■ **"Air" (Key)**

A leading title for Key, who (with Leaf) made a name for themselves with novel games. An animated movie is in the works. The music is as notable as the storyline and graphics, and quite a few fanzine circles have done their own arrangements. Other Key titles have also been big hits, like "Kanon" and "CLANNAD" ("CLANNAD" is a wide-release game, not a porno game), which are favorites among fanzine creators. The staff has done work for Tactics, and is responsible for "ONE ~ Kagayaku Kisetsu e~" and "MOON," which created their fan following.

▶ **"Kakyuusei 2" (Elf) "Rance 6" (Alice Soft)**
Elf and Alice Soft are the top developers in Tokyo and Osaka, with their new releases regularly debuting as top sellers. These two developers and F and C (Fairytale and Cocktail Soft) used to be thought of as the Three Major Houses, and are long-established developers of porno games—their games date back to the pre-Windows era of the NEC8801 and 9801 computer series. On August 24, 2004, Elf's leading series, "~kyuusei," and Alice Soft's leading series, "Rance," were released simultaneously. The resulting race for the best-selling position was dubbed the "East-West Battle."

Kanji: Kousaka, you've been here since this morning?

Kousaka: Yeah, I didn't have any classes. But I have to head back for the afternoon session. I'll see you later!

Kousaka leaves the store.

Madarame: I should have ditched my morning class too. What do you want to do, Sasahara? Want to buy two other games?

Kanji: I don't think so. I want to hang on to enough money for it in case they wind up rereleasing it (*20) soon. I guess I'll just buy one game now and then keep an eye on the website.

Madarame: Hmm, good idea. Anyway, I can just borrow the other new games from Kousaka, but I can't pass up the first-print bonus. So are you going to buy something that comes with a store bonus item (*21)?

Kanji: No, I don't need any phone cards. I'd rather buy something cheaper.

Madarame: I see. Then we should hit the used-game stores (*22).

Kanji: Used games?

30 minutes later, Sasahara and Madarame are eating lunch at a maid café.

Kanji: I'm a bit nervous.

■ **"Shirotsumesouwa" (Little Witch)**
This was the debut title from Little Witch, a new developer that caught people's attention with their high-quality sound and art. The artist is Ashito Ohyari, a fan favorite who worked on the popular console game "Kita e" under the pen name NOCCHI.

▶ **"Kimi ga Nozomu Eien" (age)**
A pure romance adventure game that started the Kimi-Nozo boom. The three companies in the Chiyoda-ku area, including age, Nitroplus (creator of "Phantom" and "Demonbane"), and Overflow (creator of "Pure Mail") are referred to as the Chiyo Coalition, and they put on events together. They and the Saitama Coalition are the most active developers.

13: First-print bonus
A bonus item that the developer includes in the first print of the video game. The bonuses can be just about anything: mousepads, desktop calendars, conceptual art illustration books, theme song CDs, and CD-ROMs of artwork are common, but some include soundtrack CDs, drama CDs, figures, side story novels, color illustration books, or pocket watches. Regular-edition and limited-edition versions are released simultaneously at different prices, and only the limited edition includes the bonus items. The first-print and limited-print runs for big titles are valued more in the collectors' market.

12: Jack-off games
A nickname for porno games that are mainly created as masturbation tools. They usually involve very little plot, and about 90% of the graphics are erotic, with an erotic scene usually appearing within the first five minutes. The games are structured as simple adventure or novel games, and involve very little gameplay. It's easy to get through the entire game quickly, which is ideal for salarymen with very little time. Most of the games fall into the masochism or humiliation categories, but there are also pure romance and moe games with stronger characterization. There are no major hits in this genre, but if the setting and graphics are good a game can consistently sell well. Most of the titles are embarrassing to say out loud. This type of game comes closest to the public image of porno games, but there are other types as well; games that focus on gameplay are called "play a lot" games, and emotionally touching stories are called "tearjerkers."

11: "Class Maid" and the other three titles are all fake games.

Madarame: Really? Is this your first time in a maid café (*23)?

Kanji: Yeah. I'm not really used to being greeted with, "Welcome home, master."

Sasahara sneaks a look at the waitress in her maid costume. Madarame catches him and smirks.

Madarame: It's not like we're in the red-light district. Think of it as an unusual café. An unusual café with a decent lunch.

Kanji: That's true. And it's not as expensive as I thought it would be.

Sasahara stops looking at the restaurant's displays and merchandise, and reads over the menu.

Madarame: It's a great place to have lunch during the week, since it's pretty empty and quiet. There aren't that many places in Akiba where you can just relax. If you come during the afternoon on weekends or holidays, you have to wait in line for a long time before you can get in. Anyway, you lucked out finding an unopened game (*24) at the used-game store. Did you get it for 5,800 yen?

Kanji: Yeah, so now I have a bit of extra money. I didn't know they sold new games at used-game stores!

Madarame: Some guys go around buying the same game from all the different

19: Pre-order
It used to be that there were long lines in front of Messe Sanoh and Sofmap in Akihabara on the day before major titles were released, because everyone wanted to get the stores' exclusive bonus items. The lines clogged the narrow sidewalks, resulting in complaints from residents and neighboring stores, so most specialty stores now accept pre-orders.

18: Mosaic error
Under Japanese law, showing male or female pubic hair is prohibited, and the artwork requires a mosaic. There are strict inspections, but sometimes a game that is missing one slips through the cracks and makes it to the market. This doesn't mean that the mosaic is missing entirely, just that one of the mosaic panels has been removed, and it's easy to miss unless you're looking very closely.

17: Recall
Voluntary recalls happen for various reasons, such as a major bug, a virus, or—most commonly—a lack of mosaic, which is usually discovered on or before the release date, after copies of the product have already been distributed. Those copies command premium prices on Internet auction sites and in used-game stores.

16: Information sites
The release date calendars in girly game magazines are only useful as a basic reference. But it's time-consuming to look through a developer's official site when you need to check more than one or two titles. That's when information sites and mailing lists that have connections with distributors and stores come in handy. They're also good resources for finding out about patches from developers. One recommended site is Depend Space (http://www.nona.dti.ne.jp/d~space/).

15: Delayed release

It's not uncommon for a porno game's release to be delayed, and sometimes the delay isn't announced until the actual release date. It's understandable when a delay happens because bugs or compatibility issues have been discovered, but some developers postpone releases because they're not satisfied with the final product, or because they didn't meet the deadline. One frequent reason for a delay is that, unlike the major corporations who make games for the average consumer, porno game companies don't have a financial cushion to fall back on. A large corporation can afford to go through a months-long debugging period after releasing a beta version, and that allows them to release their titles on time.

However, porno game developers can only afford to debug for a limited period of time before they have to print the game. They also have to send out their press releases when the games are only 40-50% complete, at which point the script and main artwork are probably still being worked on.

This is also why you need to remember to check the company websites for patches periodically.

14: Land mine

When used in the context of "land mine games," it generally refers to a crappy game, and more particularly is used for games that have good graphics or were reviewed in girly game magazines (magazines are rarely called "porno game magazines") despite having bad storylines or game systems. It's sometimes possible to identify a land mine just from the names of the developer or staff, but sometimes it's due to the artwork or a particular storyline. This isn't a very politically correct term, especially given the civil wars around the world, but it's commonly used. It's often phrased as, "Oh, I stepped on a land mine again."

stores to get the different in-store bonuses, but there's no point owning a bunch of copies of the actual game. So they sell them to the used-game stores, and since the game hasn't been opened, the store gives them a good price. It's still technically used, so it's cheaper than buying new. Sometimes the used stores wind up with a bunch of copies of the big titles when they come out, so you can get it for half the retail price on the release date. But I'm still bummed about the recall today. I bet the *tenbaichu* (*25) are having a field day.

Kanji: *"Tenbaichu"*?

Madarame: Those guys buy up limited editions or low print-run titles and then make a killing selling 'em on Yahoo auction (*26). Recalls like this are gold mines for them, even though they probably only make a few thousand yen on each copy. Maybe ten thousand, if they're lucky.

Kanji: But even though one game was recalled, that leaves 26 new releases today. That's a lot of games!

Madarame: It's a normal number for a Friday at the end of the month, though. This is the day over half of the month's titles come out! Look, here's the breakdown: Let's say there are 50 new titles every month, so that's almost 600 (*27) in a year. That's a

22: Used-game stores

The rift between the developers and the used-game stores is clearly seen in the Association of Copyright for Computer Software (ACCS), Computer Entertainment Suppliers' Association (CESA), and Japan Personal-Computer Software Association (JPSA)'s movement to reduce used software sales. The developers' rights were protected from the used software judgment, but the right to sell used software is still being evaluated. In terms of porno games, the system of store-exclusive bonus merchandise goes hand in hand with the used-game store system.

21: Store bonus item

In addition to first-print exclusive items and pre-order bonus items made by the developers, specialty stores design and manufacture bonus items to offer people who buy the product at their store. Most of these items are telephone cards, but since each store uses a different illustration, collectors buy multiple copies of the game in different stores. Large stores can offer nicer bonus gifts for big titles, like original soundtrack CDs, drama CDs, original storyline data files, body pillow covers, clocks, music boxes... In order to guarantee getting one of the items, it's safest to pre-order the game.

20: Rerelease

Two weeks is the shortest delay you can hope for. Long delays can last for two or three months.

▶ "Welcome to Pia Carot 3" (F and C FC02 Brand)

The first installment in the series was released under F and C's Cocktail Soft brand. One feature is that the player can select the waitresses' uniform. The series has a large following among the fanzine culture. The most recent sequel, "3," was released in 2001, and fans are eagerly awaiting the 4th game.

23: Maid café

Maid cafés can be traced back to the Pia Carot Restaurant, which opened in 1999 and was only in operation for a limited time. It was a theme restaurant based on the porno game "Welcome to Pia Carot!" It was a hit, and similar cosplay cafés began popping up. Akihabara's first maid café, "Cure Maid Café," opened in 2001. Between maid and cosplay cafés, there are now 17 similar stores in Akihabara (as of September 2004). Maids are one of the most popular types of character in porno games (along with nurses and shrine maidens). There are countless maid games, but not that many "maid café" games. One such game is "Let's Have Tea in Akiba!" (by Angel Smaile).

lot, since they each cost 9,000 yen. And that's not counting all the DVD-player games (*28) coming out these days.

Kanji: Do porno games sell that well?

Madarame: No way. Back in the day a game had to move 10,000 copies to be considered a big hit. Now they call it a hit if it sells 5,000 copies. Plus they cost more to make now, since it's normal to include voice tracks. Sure, some titles sell 50,000 or even 100,000 units, but they're *really* rare, and it's not like the porno game user base is very big. Probably 70% of the games get sold in Akiba and in Nipponbashi (*29), in Osaka. But there're probably only about 30,000 people in Japan who play porno games regularly and come down to the electronics district to buy them on Fridays and Saturdays. And of all of them, except for the businessmen who get bonuses some months, most people can only buy two or three games a month. So plenty of titles just don't sell. You saw the dump bin in the stores, didn't you?

Kanji: Some of the games in there were going for only a third or a quarter of the regular price. There were even a few that were only 980 yen. And I don't even want to think about one of them—I ran out and bought it on the release date a couple

---

30: Fanzine shop

Fanzine specialty stores (or stores with floors dedicated to fanzines), including Tora no Ana, K-BOOKS, Mandarake, Messa Sanoh, and Melon Books, extend from the end of the Akihabara electronics district to the Chuou-dori. After the summer and winter Comiket, the area is flooded with people who couldn't get their hands on the latest releases.

29: Nipponbashi

The electronics district in Osaka, always called "Nipponbashi" instead of "Nihonbashi." It's similar to Akihabara in that the otaku elements have expanded, and it's turning into a hobby town. Also called "Ponbashi."

28: DVD-player game

A game played on a DVD player instead of on your computer. It can also be played on the PlayStation 2, which means porn games can be played in households without a computer. Most of the titles are ported from the computer versions, but there are a few original titles being announced as well.

27: 600 titles per year

There were 289 titles released in the first half of the year in 2004 (if the same titles are released via different media, they only count once). It looks like there will be roughly 600 titles this year as well.

26: Yahoo auction

The leading Internet auction site in Japan. Other major sites include "Rakuten Flea Market" and "BIDDERS."

25: Tenbaichu (Second market seller)
A term that evolved from the popular BBS site terminology for "2 channel," *chuubou* (which literally means kitchen). When written with different kanji, *chuubou* becomes another word (literally, junior high student), and it is used to refer to people who speak or behave immaturely.

24: Unopened product
These usually cost about 500 yen less than a brand-new copy. They don't include the specialty-store exclusive items and giveaway posters, so it's a good buy if you only want to enjoy the game. They're generally sold out by Friday afternoon, so if you're looking for unopened new games, you should go around noon.

▶ **"Let's Have Tea in Akiba!" (Angel Smaile)**
A romantic adventure game where the main character inherits a run-down café in Akihabara and turns it into a maid café with the help of four young potential wives. It's the ultimate porno game combo: Akiba + maid café + Lolita.

months ago for 6,800 yen, and it was in there for 2,980 yen!

Madarame: Think of it as an investment! Porno game fans are the few and the proud! There aren't a lot of us, but the games are the heart of otaku media right now. Look at Comic-Fest! Most of the fanzines are based on porno games instead of anime, and they're making a lot more TV anime series that are based on the games. They're the core of Akiba multimedia—well, manga is, too—and there are porno gamers working in the anime, manga, and light novel industries. So the games are influencing their creative work, and indirectly influencing hundreds more consumers than you'd think. It's not a waste to invest in the industry that supports the entire Japanese subculture!

Kanji: How is it supporting the industry if we buy games used?

Madarame: Next we're off to a fanzine shop (*30). Since we have some leftover cash, we should check out a few fan-made games (*31). We need to invest in the youths who will lead us to the culture of tomorrow! Let's go, Sasahara!

Kanji: Hey, wait up!

Maid/waitress: Have a good day, master.

Sasahara bows to the waitress and chases after Madarame. They disappear into Akihabara. It's 2:00 P.M. Akihabara on Friday is still blisteringly hot.

▶ **"Fate/stay night" (TYPE-MOON)**
Released in January 2004, this was the corporate game debut for TYPE-MOON, the group that created the overwhelmingly popular fan-made game "Tsuki Hime." The developer's online store sold out of pre-orders in 30 minutes; pre-orders alone accounted for 100,000 units. They were a force to be reckoned with at the summer 2004 Comiket.

Fate
stay night

31: Fan-made games
Fan-made computer games can be produced on a low budget if you burn the CD-Rs at home. They can be made more cheaply than offset fanzines, so lately it's becoming a common hobby. The price is about 1,000 yen in stores, but it can be as low as 500 yen or as high as 2,000 yen. They vary from illustration collections to adventure games. Recently, some fan-made games have been packaged, although they're not that similar to commercial products. There are times when industry professionals get involved and make high-quality games, and many pros like TYPE-MOON got their start with fan-made games.

Note: The information and opinions listed in the notes and captions are not official comments from the developers.

Circle Entrance

People who will be selling fanzines at an event are given tickets to get into the hall before everyone else so they can set up their booth. It's tough to start working so early in the morning, but you get the satisfaction of fully participating in the event.

Mad Dash

A mad dash involves running to the circles you came for as soon as the event opens up. However, running in the hall is against the rules. If you bump into someone or fall, it can result in serious injury.

Loop

Some popular circles allow you to buy only one fanzine at a time. They do this so the fanzine gets to the most people who want it. But some people just keep getting in line after they buy it. This is very impolite.

Regular Attendee

A regular attendee is someone who attends an event only to buy things. Unlike circles, they don't have to create fanzines or apply to have a booth. Being a regular attendee means being willing to endure the long lines while you wait for the hall to open, and then lining up again to buy fanzines.

Wall Circle

Popular circles that have regular fans get crowded, so they get areas near the wall. Most of them are placed there based on their past sales and lines.

Winter Fest

In "Genshiken," the summer Comic-Fest is held during the three days of *obon*, and the winter fest is held at the end of December. You can spend New Year's reading fanzines. The real-world Comiket is also held around those times.

THE SOCIETY FOR THE STUDY OF MODERN VISUAL CULTURE

Kio Shimoku

Special Bonus—The Author Reveals Extra Information About the Characters

"Genshiken" volume 1 included profiles of all the club members. Each character's answers refer to anime and games that do not exist. In this chapter, the author provides a detailed look at how those titles were created.

1:

All of the characters' birth dates and blood types came from the first "Gundam Fortune-telling Book." I selected the mobile suit that fit the character's personality, and then worked backwards to determine their birthday and blood type. Kanji is Ball.

2:

HUNTER x HUNTER

Panther is the name of a German tank. But there's no real reason I chose that name. When you read plastic model magazines, these things just start to come naturally. German tanks are popular among plastic tank models.

3:

Berserk

4:

Patlabor the Movie

5:

Dragon Quest III

Sasahara likes it because of its flexibility in creating characters, and because it completes the trilogy.

6:

THE KING OF FIGHTERS '95

7:

Iori Yagami (KOF Series)

All of Kanji's favorite fight game characters are the same as mine. He's

a main character who doesn't have strong traits of his own, so I just listed what I like. It's mostly "good-looking but slightly crazy guys" or "sexy girls."

8:

Mai Shiranui (Fatal Fury Series)

I took Mai Shiranui and added Mamoru Shiranui from "Dokaben" and used

Mamoru's kanji character from "Sister Princess." There's no real rhyme or reason to it.

9:

Zabel (Vampire Series)

Eric Zabel is a name of an actual cyclist. Any gamer who sees his name would immediately think of this character.

10:

Basara the Beheader (Samurai Spirits Series)

On pages 92 and 95 of volume 2, Kanji and Madarame's lines are from Basara and Nakoruru's battle. I used to play those characters with my friends.

MADARAME HARUNOBU

PROFILE

HARUNOBU MADARAME
BORN FEBRUARY 25TH
BLOOD TYPE O

*FAVORITE
MANGA*
BE-BOP-HELL-SING
YOTAROO'S SAD SONG

*FAVORITE
ANIME*
MOBILE SUITS T-GANGARU
DOREMI-CHAN
YUCKO!
THE ADVENTURES OF
DORA THE SPACE PIRATE
SPIRITED AFAR

*FAVORITE
VIDEO GAMES*
THE DIARY OF KAGERO
NINJA ADVENTURES
ENCHO
SHINOBI RETURNS
THE OUTLAW KANKIRO

*FAVORITE
FIGHT GAME
CHARACTERS*
KINAKO BERETTA
TARURUN

*THESE ARE THE
CHARACTER'S CHOICES AND
DO NOT NECESSARILY
REFLECT THE AUTHOR'S TASTES.*

1:
Zeong

2:
HELLSING
I just copied the volume 2 inside-cover parody wholesale.

3:
Gundam, directed by Tomino
Here, too. In the manga, we referred to "Gundam" by its real title, but we used "Gangaru" here because all the other titles were jumbled and we wanted it to match.

4:
Ojamajo Doremi
This is a combination of "Ojarumaru" and "Ojamanga Yamada-kun."

5:
Yadamon

6:
Adventures of Space Pirate Mito

7:
Spirited Away
All of the anime listed basically have to do with a Lolita complex. By listing them, he's sort of making his own

characterization, isn't he? But I do like all of the titles he chose. Oh, but "Spirited Away" might be too worldly...

8:
Kokumeikan Shinshou Kagerou

9:
Rittai Ninja Katsugeki Tenchu Shinobi Gaisen

10:
Samurai Shodown III: Blades of Blood
This is my favorite of the Samurai Shodown series, too.

11:
Yellow Nakoruru (Samurai Shodown Series)
This is another Lolita character. There is no

particular explanation for why he likes the yellow version.

12:
Bulleta (Vampire Savior)

13:
Marurun (Waku Waku 7)
I'm moe for Mugi-chan. Enough said.

1:
She's Elmeth.
She's actually not a good match with Gyan. (laughs)

2:

Ike! Inachuu Takkubu [Go! Inachu Ping-Pong Club]
She probably read this in her boyfriend's room in high school. She really liked it, so she reread it several times. But she probably doesn't realize that she and Ohno are similar to "Inachu's" Kyoko and Kamiya-san. I didn't make the connection until later. It's true! But I did imagine Kousaka, Saki, and Madarame as Takeda, Kyoko, and Maeno.

3:

Ohke no Monshou [Emblem of Royalty]
She probably didn't read it all the way through. (laughs) She read parts of it here and there at her friends' houses.

4:
She probably saw some when she was a little girl, but she stopped watching as she got older. Well, that's normal. (laughs)

5:
She said this sarcastically, and probably doesn't really like it.

Saki Kasukabe / Makoto Kosaka

PROFILE

MAKOTO KOUSAKA
BORN FEBRUARY 2ND
BLOOD TYPE B

FAVORITE
MANGA
THE MYSTERIOUS
ADVENTURES OF DADA

FAVORITE
ANIME
PRETTY MUCH
ANYTHING

FAVORITE
VIDEO GAMES
FULL ARMOR

STREET MASTER 2

DRACULINA HUNTER

FAVORITE
FIGHT GAME
CHARACTERS
JULIETTE
SAKAMOTO
TAKIKEN
GOKI

*THESE ARE THE
CHARACTER'S CHOICES AND
DO NOT NECESSARILY
REFLECT THE AUTHOR'S TASTES.

1:
I didn't know that there's a voice actress by the same name. I'm so sorry. Kousaka only had a last name at first, and I picked his name for this page. I wondered why Saki only ever calls him by his last name; I thought maybe his name was a girly kind of guy's name. I was happy that it was a voice actress who shared the name.

2:
He's Gyan. Manga characters are designed to have specific personalities, so when you work backwards, all of their blood types are strange. Type A is the most common Japanese blood type, but Kugayama is the only one who has it. Even Kanji is type B.

3:
Jojo's Bizarre Adventure
I thought this kind of powerful manga was perfect for Kousaka. Very straightforward and no-nonsense.

4:
Armored Core
It's not jumbled much.

5:
Street Fighter II
"Air Master" is mixed into the title.

6:
Vampire Hunter
The female characters of the "Vampire" series

change after "Savior," so he likes the "Hunter" game preceding it.

7:
Ryu, Ken, Goki (Street Fighter Series)
He usually plays with the main characters. He likes action games. Of course, he likes "Puyopuyo," too. (laughs) He does play major RPGs as well.

8:
Julietta Sakamoto (Air Master)
She is not a fighting game character. She is a character from the manga series "Air Master." If this manga was made into a fighting game... I would like to use Jones Lee.

1:

Gundam

She was supposed to be Zock at first, but I mixed up blood types B and O and she became a Gundam. But she seems suited to being a Gundam, so it all worked out in the end. (laughs)

2:

Chinmoku no Kantai

Now it would probably be "Zipang."

3:

All of the Gundam series

...is what she would like to say. Now, she would say that "Gundam" with no older male characters is not "Gundam."

4:

Samurai Spirits

She must really like it. I wonder if she played it in the U.S. Has it been released there?

5:

Yagu Jubei (Samurai Spirits Series)

It's combined with the "Jubei-chan" anime series. Lovely eye-patch.

6:

Wanfu (Samurai Spirits Series)

An old man with a queue. Konigstiger is a German tank. But I was a bit surprised when he turned into a character who tosses rock pillars around. After that, his disappearance was only to be expected. He doesn't seem to be returning any time soon. [NOTE: the tank's full name is "Panzerkampfwagen VI Ausf. B 'Konigstiger'"]

7:

Earthquake (Samurai Spirits Series)

She likes him, too? He came back recently.

8:

Zangief (Street Fighter Series)

"Zangula" is the infamous typo. The "Urya Up" attack is still valid in my book.

Kanako Ohno / Souichiro Tanaka/Mitsunori Kugayama

1:
Gun Canon

2:
The Five Star Stories
When you look at his list, he seems to prefer high-quality series. He's just acting cool.

3:
Laputa, Castle in the Sky

4:
Future Boy Conan
When you hear "Conan," you think "future boy." A few years ago on a late-night TV show, a young model said, "Conan is a detective," and a comedian was visibly upset. I understand that feeling.

5:
Tactics Ogre
When you hear "ogre," what do you think of? That's right. Baki's dad.

6:
Vagrant Story
Because "vagabond" and "vagrant" mean the same thing.

7:
Kizuato
If they're good-quality, he likes erotic games, too. But writing it down is kind of perverted for him. These days, though, liking erotic games has become the norm.

PROFILE

SOUICHIRO TANAKA
BIRTHDAY DECEMBER 22ND
BLOOD TYPE AB

FAVORITE MANGA
THE SEVEN STAR STORIES

FAVORITE ANIME
RYUNOS: THE CASTLE IN THE SKY
CONAN THE BOY FROM THE FUTURE

FAVORITE VIDEO GAMES
YUUJIRO TACTIC
THE STORY OF MR. STUPID

FAVORITE FIGHT GAME CHARACTERS
DR. HAYWOOD

PROFILE

MITSUNORI KUGAYAMA
BIRTHDAY JUNE 29TH
BLOOD TYPE A

FAVORITE MANGA
ANMAN BALL

FAVORITE ANIME
FUN WITH THE TARURUN FAMILY (BEFORE THE THEME SONG CHANGED)

FAVORITE VIDEO GAMES
EXITGE

FAVORITE FIGHT GAME CHARACTERS
THE LOVELY YOOGA TISETTE

8:
Geese Howard (Fatal Fury)
I mixed the name with Duck King of the same game. I like Geese, but my friend used him a lot so I didn't use him much. Counter throw.

9:
GM (Land Combat Type)

10:
Azumanga Daioh
He likes fun, cute series.

11:
Fun with Mumin Family
When the opening changed, I was shocked, too!

12:
Waku Waku 7

13:
I–I'm sorry. I don't remember what this was based on. I think "Pretty Yoga" is mixed in there, but I'm just not sure. Maybe Dhalsim became lovely?

14:
Tesse (Waku Waku 7)

About the Author

Kio Shimoku was born in 1974. In 1994 his debut work, Ten No Ryoiki, received second place in the "Afternoon Shiki Prize" contest. Other past works include Kageriybikii, Yonensei, and Gonensei, all of which appeared in Afternoon magazine.
He has been working on Genshiken since 2002.

Genshiken Official Book

Supervised by **Kio Shimoku**

Compiled by **Katsumi Ishitsuka**

Edited by **Koichi Yuri**

Written by **Yuka Minakawa, Takashi Umemura, Yasuhiro Muroi, KASIN, Hideki Kobubu, Ryu Mitsui, Kio Shimoku, Katsumi Ishitsuka**

Photography by **Kanako Hamada, Yoshihiro Kamiya (Kodansha Ltd.)**

By courtesy of **Keisuke Murakami ("Afternoon"), Naoko Okabe ("Afternoon"), Ken Akamatsu, "Weekly Shonen Magazine", Hidemi Moriya, Kazuaki Morijiri (Genco, Inc.), Michiko Yokote, Takaya Ibira (Showgate Inc.), Mariko Hubota**

Japanese is a tricky language for most Westerners, and translation is often more art than science. For your edification and reading pleasure, here are notes on some of the places where we could have gone in a different direction in our translation of the work, or where a Japanese cultural reference is used.

Gangaru, Kaira-san, and Hinno, page 118

This is a reference to Seira-san from the series *Gundam*. "Hinno" is a play on the name of the director, Yoshiyuki Tomino. In Tomino's name, "tomi" means "wealthy" or "in abundance," while the "hin" in Hinno means "poor."

Romu-chan, page 118

This is a reference to Lum, the heroine from the anime series "Urusei Yatsura."

Studio Circus, page 118

This refers to Pierrot (formerly known as Studio Pierrot), an animation studio. They worked on "Urusei Yatsura" until episode 129.

Hana and Dirty Twins, page 118

This is a reference to Kei from the series "Dirty Pair."

Sunset, page 118

This is a reference to animation studio Sunrise, who worked on "Dirty Pair."

Q-ko-san and Ikkoku Hall, page 118

This refers to Kyoko-san from "Maison Ikkoku."

Buru, Gangaru Double, page 119

This is a reference to Elpeo Puru from *Gundam ZZ*. She refers to the main character, Judau Ashta, as "onii-chan."

Cream Pumpkin, page 119

This is a reference to the series "Cream Lemon," one of the notorious porno anime of the '80s.

rtan X-ko, page 119

...s is a reference to "Project A-ko," a comedic anime with action and ...tire.

Bass, page 119

This is a reference to Randy William Bass, known as the legendary helper of Japanese baseball. He played on the Hanshin Tigers as the first baseman.

Chuo University, page 121

Chuo University is a private university in Tokyo. Shiiou University, where *Genshiken* is set, is apparently based on Chuo University.

Shopper, page 137

Kasukabe is referring to the high-quality store-brand bags you get when you buy from a boutique. In Japan, you call those "shoppers." (Think of bags from Neiman Marcus, etc.)

Evo and Sunshine, page 139

Sasahara is referring to Sunshine City, a building complex located in east Ikebukuro. The "Comic Revolution" is held here, which in the Genshiken world they refer to as "Comic Evolution." (Madarame shortens it by calling it "Evo.")

Gundam Fortune-telling, page 192

Gundam Fortune-telling is a series of books published in Japan that determine your type of mobile suit based on your birth date and blood type.

Ball, page 192

Ball is a fictional weapon that appears in the *Gundam* series.

Dokaben, page 192

Dokaben is a baseball manga that was serialized in the 1970s and early 1980s.

Hellsing, page 193
The inside covers of the *HELLSING* manga featured a parody comic under the dust jacket cover.

Ojarumaru and Ojamanga Yamada-kun, page 193
"Ojarumaru" is an NHK Education TV anime series that started in 1998. "Ojamanga Yamada-kun" is an anime series from 1980.

Yadamon, page 193
"Yadamon" is an NHK Education TV anime that aired from 1992 to 1993. There are a total of 170 episodes.

Kagero: Deception II, page 193
"Kagero: Deception II" is a PlayStation game released by TECMO.

Kinako, page 193
Kinako is a combination of the word *kiiro* ("yellow" in Japanese) and the first two syllables of Nakoruru.

Waku Waku 7, page 193
"Waku Waku 7" is a SUNSOFT fighting game. It was released as an arcade game in the US in 1996.

Zipang, page 196
Zipang is a manga about a Japanese naval ship.

Conan, page 197
The model mentioned here was referring to *Detective Conan*, known as *Case Closed* in the U.S.

Baki, page 197
Baki refers to "Grappler Baki." Baki's father, Yujiro Hanma, was nicknamed "the ogre" in the fighting world.

The following four pages contain reproductions of full-color trading cards created for *Kujibiki Unbalance*. The cards were bound into the Japanese edition of the *Genshiken Official Book*.

KUJIBIKI UNBALANCE Trading Cards

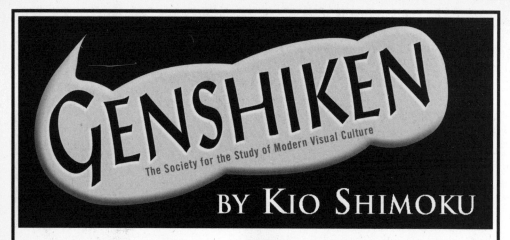

GENSHIKEN

The Society for the Study of Modern Visual Culture

BY KIO SHIMOKU

ARE YOU OTAKU?

It's the spring of freshman year, and Kanji Sasahara is in a quandary. Should he fulfill his long-cherished dream of joining an otaku club? Saki Kasukabe also faces a dilemma. Can she ever turn her boyfriend, anime fanboy Kousaka, into a normal guy? Kanji triumphs where Saki fails, when both Kanji and Kousaka sign up for Genshiken: The Society for the Study of Modern Visual Culture.

Undeterred, Saki chases Kousaka through various activities of the club, from cosplay and comic conventions to video gaming and collecting anime figures—all the while discovering more than she ever wanted to know about the humorous world of the Japanese otaku!

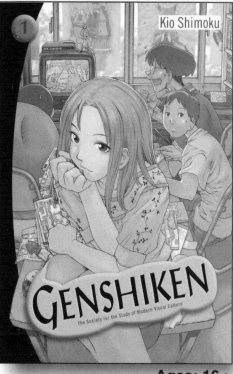

Ages: 16+

Special extras in each volume! Read them all!

STORY BY KIO SHIMOKU
ART BY KOUME KEITO

FROM THE PAGES OF *GENSHIKEN*!

The Genshiken gang have long obsessed over a manga called *Kujibiki Unbalance*, the story of an average boy who becomes class president at a ritzy academy. Now *Kujibiki Unbalance* is a real-life manga for every fan's enjoyment!

• The eagerly awaited spin-off to the bestselling *Genshiken* series!

Special extras in each volume! Read them all!

ALIVE

STORY BY TADASHI KAWASHIMA
ART BY TOKA ADACHI

SMART SCIENCE-FICTION SUSPENSE

Millions of people worldwide have taken their own lives, victims of a lethal alien pandemic visited upon the Earth.

But a group of Tokyo teens has somehow survived and now, facing a devastated world, must ask questions they never thought they'd have to ask:

Why did they abandon us?
Will we be next?
Why are we alive?

Special extras in each volume! Read them all!

VISIT WWW.DELREYMANGA.COM TO:
- Read sample pages
- View release date calendars for upcoming volumes
- Sign up for Del Rey's free manga e-newsletter
- Find out the latest about new Del Rey Manga series

RATING   OT AGES 16+

DEL REY MANGA デルレイ

The Otaku's Choice™

BY HITOSHI IWAAKI

THEY DESCEND FROM THE SKIES.
THEY HAVE A HUNGER FOR HUMAN FLESH.

They are parasites and they are everywhere. They must take control of a human host to survive, and once they do, they can assume any deadly form they choose.

But they haven't taken over everyone! High school student Shin is resisting the invasion— battling for control of his own body against an alien parasite committed to thwart his plans to warn humanity of the horrors to come.

- *Now published in authentic right-to-left format!*
- *Featuring an all-new translation!*

Special extras in each volume! Read them all!

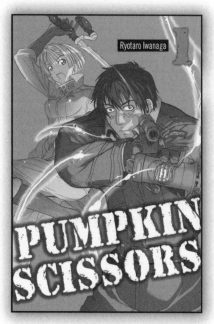

止まれ

TOMARE!

[STOP!]

You're going the wrong way!

**Manga is a completely different type
of reading experience.**

**To start at the *beginning*,
go to the *end*!**

That's right! Authentic manga is read the
traditional Japanese way—from right to left.
Exactly the *opposite* of how American books are
read. It's easy to follow: Just go to the other end
of the book, and read each page—and each
panel—from right side to left side, starting at the
top right. Now you're experiencing manga as it
was meant to be!